2/3

Don-M

Plate 1. Sugar bush hexagon (162 cm x 126 cm). Medallion layout. Maretha Fourie.

MARETHA FOURIE
PROTEA DESIGNS
FOR PIECING
& QUILTING

TAFELBERG

Acknowledgements. The pleasure I have had in preparing this book was directly dependent on the support of family members and friends who were interested and fellow enthusiasts who were willing to experiment with new patterns and ideas. There are also those quilting professionals whom I met during my visit to the United States whose knowledge and enthusiasm for this art form assured me that it would be worthwhile to create something typically South African.

Special thanks to the following people:

K'oosie Uys, textile artist and author of two books on embroidering South African wild flowers, who was a wonderful teacher and inspired me to explore a new field. I also thank her for making her embroidery designs available for quilting designs.

Cela Kvevli, graphic artist, who volunteered to make the drawings and eventually became indispensably part of the book.

Prof. Mattie Jooste, emeritus professor in Home Economics, for years of encouragement and help.

My husband, Marius, for endless patience and help in many ways.

Cover design by G&G, Cape Town
Quilt on cover by Maretha Fourie
Drawings by Cela Kvevli
Photographs by Faan van Tonder
Set in 10½ on 12 pt Triumvirate
by Diatype Setting, Cape Town
Colour separation by
Syreline Process, Cape Town
Printed and bound by
Toppan Printing Company (H.K.) Ltd,
Hong Kong
First edition 1984

ISBN 0 624 02257 9

Plate 2. *Top:* Protea-octagon (103 cm x 103 cm; 27 cm blocks). *Protea longifolia* and protea buds pieced according to inlay method and appliquéd on to background. Irene van Tonder. *Bottom:* Back view of Protea octagon.

CONTENTS

Introduction, 6

I Block designs, 8

II Fabric, the use of colour and equipment, 26

III The size, layout and planning of a quilt top, 32

IV Piecing, 44

V Quilting, 50

VI Finishing edges, 75

VII Signing and care of quilts, 78

Bibliography, 79

Index, 79

LIST OF PLATES

1 Sugar bush hexagon, 2

2 Protea-octagon, 4

3 Protea-diamonds, 7

4 Protea Paisley, 11

5 *Protea punctata*, 17

6 Fynbos, 21

7 Leucospermum rainbow, 29

8 Swing-glass, 34

9 Centre-pieces of wall quilts, 38

10 Protea Brillianté, 43

11 Centre-piece of a medallion quilt, 47

12 Centre-piece of a bed quilt, 49

13 Part of a bed quilt design, 53

14 *Protea rubropilosa*, 76

15 *Protea barbigera*, 77

16 Border patterns for quilting, 77

INTRODUCTION

In the search for typically South African quilting designs the protea — our country's beautiful national flower — is the natural choice. For though we cannot boast a quilting tradition sprung from generations past, this form of needle art is today pursued by such a great number of enthusiasts that it justifies the development of a distinctly South African character.

The greatest variety of proteas in the world is found in the Republic. The firm, squarely-built protea flowers arem particularly suited for stylized designs in quilting patterns and blocks. The leaves are stiff and leathery and usually grow so densely that they conceal the stems.

Single flowers are found at the end of the stem in a variety of shapes — elongated, cylindrical, diamond-shaped, triangular, even round. Their shapes also change during development, from bud to half-open to fully-open flower. All these characteristics make the proteas particularly suitable for piecing, appliquéing and quilting.

In this book, ten protea species and one protea bud have been used to create eleven basic block designs, and one flower of the genus leucospermum was used to design an overall hexagonal pattern.

The motifs for the quilting designs consist of proteas as well as other typical Cape flowers ("fynbos") related to proteas in their natural habitat, growth and looks. As the original flower shapes have been simplified for quilting designs, only common names have been used to identify the different species.

A comprehensive explanation on how to use the patterns is included, along with suggestions of suitable fabrics and examples of how to adapt the patterns to make a variety of articles. Stress, though, should be laid on your own original combinations and adaptations. The sixteen colourplates have been specially chosen to illustrate use of the block patterns and layouts.

Piecing and quilting are creative activities, embracing both work and relaxation. Once the technical problems have been mastered, their calming influence can transform quiet working hours into works of art.

These patterns and the technical information are presented in such a way that everybody who loves the textile arts will be able to create something typically South African which can bring great pleasure — even to the next generation. For the quilting enthusiast new doors of creativity will be opened.

The patterns can be successfully used by the weaver, carpet maker and lead glass artist.

Plate 3. PROTEA-DIAMONDS (Amish). *Top left: Protea grandiceps* (88 cm x 88 cm). Maretha Fourie (piecing). June Kruger (quilting). *Top right: Protea cynaroides* (100 cm x 100 cm). Marie Wagner. *Bottom left: Protea lacticolor* (66 cm x 102 cm). Olive Hiemstra (piecing). June Kruger (quilting). *Bottom right: Protea lacticolor* (75 cm x 75 cm). Maretha Fourie (piecing). June Kruger (quilting).

I BLOCK DESIGNS

UNDERSTANDING THE DESIGNS

Each pattern page contains an 18 cm x 18 cm block design, a brief description of the protea and a simplified sketch. This sketch at the top of the page shows the pattern pieces and their symbols and indicates the specific order for piecing them together.

The blocks are textured to give the worker an idea of the choice of fabric. Seamlines between pieces, shown by dotted lines, should also help the worker in making her own drawing of the block. One dot represents one square on the paper. No seam allowances have been made. The proteas are placed either straight or diagonally on the block.

The degree of difficulty of each pattern is indicated on the pattern page by a star system: one for an easy pattern; up to three for a difficult one.

Before drawing a pattern from the block design, choose the correct size for the article you plan to make — 18, 27 or 36 cm. Use squared or isometric paper pads marked in 5 mm, which can be bought at stationery shops, or a 1 cm grid, available at needlework shops. The 7,5 mm grid has been printed in the back of the book. (Also see front for 1 cm and isometric grids.) All sizes may be ordered from the addresses below. Transfer the drawing onto your pattern block. Start by copying the outlines, locate the centre of the drawing by halving the lines and draw in the inner detail.

The top sketch has a symbol for every pattern piece. The letters designate the parts of the protea motive — L for leaves, B for bracts, H for flower-head and G for the background. The method and order in which the piecing should be done is explained next to the sketch. Each worker can choose her own order as well as the method she prefers.

Piecing of proteas can be done either by the single-seam or American block method, or by the inlay or English method, or else by a combination of both. Pieced flower-heads following the inlay method can be appliquéd on to the background, or the background can be pieced. Two patterns, namely the *Protea caffra* and the protea bud, are pieced according to the log-cabin method. One pattern, the leucospermum, can be pieced only by the inlay method. The recommended method is given next to the top sketch.

The protea motif must always be pieced, while the background can either be pieced or treated as a single piece of fabric on which the protea is to be appliquéd. Please note that the fabric underneath the protea must be cut away after the appliquéing has been done.

Squared paper in square sizes 5 mm, 7,5 mm and 1 cm, as well as isometric paper, may be ordered from the following addresses:

Pickles and Patchwork*
P.O. Box 89456
Lyndhurst
2106

Tel. (011) 6083825

Hammond & Co.*
Sew-Ezi Haberdashery
P.O. Box 9846
34 Troye Street
Johannesburg
2000

Tel. (011) 291594

Nettleton & Els (Pty) Ltd.
Commercial Printers
P.O. Box 310
Johannesburg
2000

Tel. (011) 3317537

*Accessories are also available at these addresses.

Squared paper in the 5 mm square size is also commercially available at stationery shops, whereas the 1 cm size can be bought as pattern designing paper at needlework shops. Isometric paper may be bought from either. Isometric and 5 mm square size working grids have been printed in the front and a 7,5 mm grid in the back of the book for your convenience. These grids can be extended by pasting together two or more photocopies or by tracing and adding squares. *Note:* The patterns in this book were all designed on a 5 mm grid.

PROTEA BARBIGERA*

The bearded protea, with its beautiful powder puff mass of white hairs within the soft pink, red or even pale yellow or deep cream-coloured bracts, is one of the most exquisite proteas. The flower is offset against grey-green foliage.

Piecing order for the single-seam method (See p. 44)

1 [(H1 + H3) + G1] + (G3 + B1) + (G5 + B3)
2 (G7 + L1) + G9
3 Step 1 + step 2
4 Repeat for the other side.

5 Sew the diagonal seam from corner to corner by hand.

The inlay method is not recommended for this block because the pattern pieces are relatively large. The single-seam method is easily sewn.

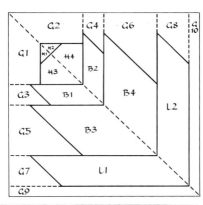

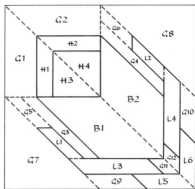

PROTEA LONGIFOLIA**

An exceptionally attractive protea. The pointed bracts are ivory or apple-green, tinged with reddish-brown or pink. The fluffy white mass of woolly flowers culminates in a black point. The yellow-green leaves are smooth and very long and narrow.

Piecing order for the single-seam method (See p. 44)

1 (G1 + H1 + H3)

2 (G5 + L1) + G3 + B1

3 (L3 + G11) + (G9 + L5)

4 (Steps 3 + 2) + step 1 + G7

5 Repeat for the other side.

6 Sew the diagonal seam from corner to corner by hand.

Piecing order for the inlay method (See p. 46)
For this method H3 and H4 can become one piece as shown in the pattern block. A fabric with printed flower motif is especially suitable for this pattern piece.

1 H1 + H3 + B1 + (L1 + L3 + L5)

2 Repeat for the other side.

Appliqué leaves and flower-head on to the background.

Plate 4. Protea Paisley (190 cm x 54 cm). Elmarie de Jager (piecing and quilting). June Kruger (quilting). *Top right: Protea punctata* (27 cm block). *Bottom right: Protea cynaroides* (27 cm block).

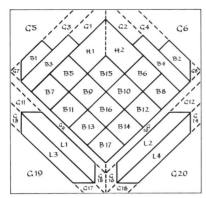

PROTEA CYNAROIDES**

The spectacular 'giant protea' with its flower-head of 15 to 30 cm across is probably the best known of all proteas. The white, soft-pink or deep crimson-coloured bracts embrace the central snowy peak of hairy flowers. The leaves are hairless and have a distinct stalk.

Piecing order for the single-seam method (See p. 44)

1 G5 + (G7 + B1 + G3) + (B3 + G1)

2 Repeat for the other side.

3 G19 + (G13 + L3 + G17) + (G11 + L1 + G15) + G9

4 Repeat for the other side.

5 (B17 + B14) + (B13 + B16) + (B11 + B9) + (B7 + B5)

6 (B12 + B8) + (B10 + B6) + (B15 + H2 + H1)

7 Steps 6 + 5 + 4 + 3 + 2 + 1

Piecing order for the inlay method (See p. 46)

1 L3 + L1, L2 + L4

2 Same order as steps 5 and 6 above + (B3 + B1) + (B4 + B2)

Appliqué leaves and flower-head on to the background.

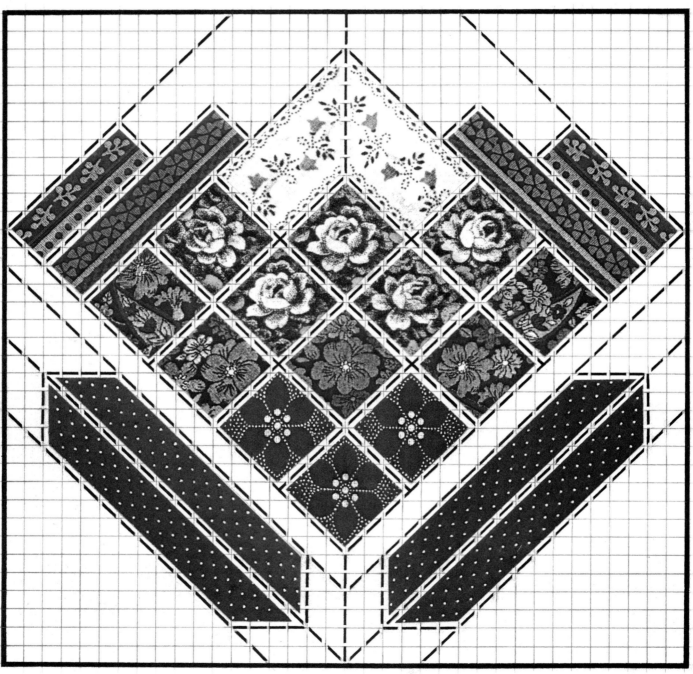

12

PROTEA NERIIFOLIA***

This was one of the first plants from Southern Africa to be described by early travellers. It has oblong flowers, ranging from deep pink to pale salmon with silky sheen, furry tips forming a cup in which the hairy pink flowers with reddish-purple tips are set. The leaves are usually long and narrow with a velvety texture.

Piecing order for the single-seam method (See p. 44)

1 G1 + H1 + B1 + B5 + B9

2 G3 + B3 + B7

3 Step 1 + step 2 + G5 + L3

4 (G7 + L1) + step 3 + G11 + G9

5 Repeat for the other side.

Sew the diagonal seam from corner to corner by hand.

Piecing order for the inlay method (See p. 46)
For this method H1 + H2 and B9 + B10 need not have a diagonal seam.

1 (B3 + B1) + (B7 + B5)

2 Repeat for other side.

3 Piece in (H1 + H2) and (B9 + B10)

4 (L1 + L3) + (L2 + L4) + steps 1 + 2 + 3

Appliqué leaves and flower-head on to the background.

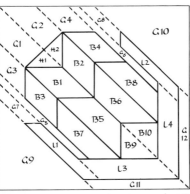

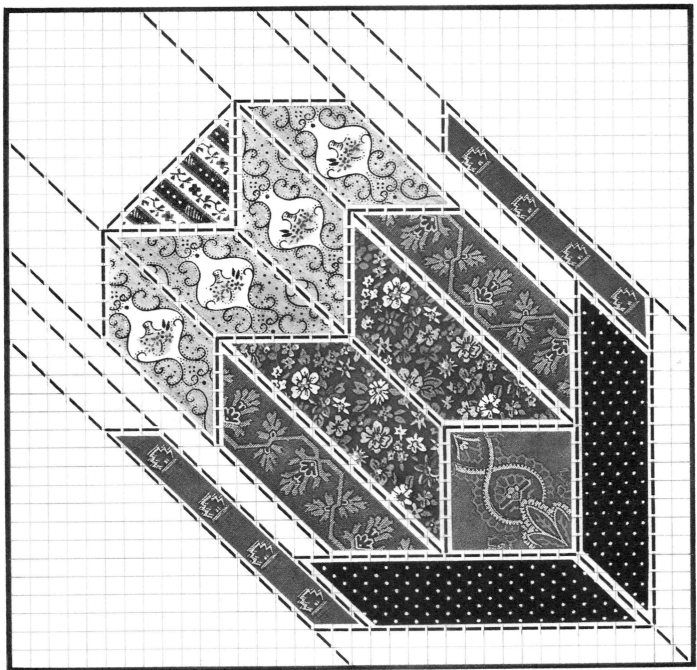

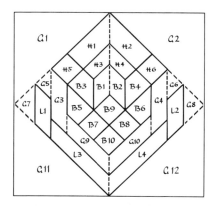

PROTEA LACTICOLOR***

This delicate, glowing flower-head is mostly creamy white or a delightful silvery pink with a silky fringe on the bracts. As the flower opens up the bracts are pushed wide open to reveal a mass of pinkish-cream hair within. The leaves are dark blue-green with a leathery texture.

Piecing order for the single-seam method (See p. 44)

1 (B10 + B8) + (B9 + B7)

2 (H5 + B3 + B5) + (H1 + H3 + B1)

3 Repeat for the other side.

4 Step 1 + step 2 + step 3 + G9 + G3 + L3 + (L1 + G5) + G7

5 Repeat for the other side.

6 The above + G1 + G2 + G11 + G12

Piecing order for the inlay method (See p. 46)

1 (B10 + B8) + (B7 + B9)

2 (B5 + B3 + B1) + (B2 + B4 + B6)

3 (H5 + H1 + H3) + (H4 + H2 + H6)

4 Steps 1 + 2 + 3

5 (L1 + L3) + (L4 + L2)

Appliqué leaves and flower-head on to the background. A stem can be appliquéd between flower-head and leaves. On the block pattern H5 + H1 and H4 + H2 are shown as two pieces with a striped fabric appliquéd on to each piece to form a border.

PROTEA GRANDICEPS**

This is a very rare protea, growing high in the mountains of the Cape. With its 10 cm long coral-red flower-heads, it is probably one of the prettiest of all proteas. The tips of the bracts have a fringe of long silky hair embracing the flower-head. The blue-green leaves are wide and oval-shaped, edged with a red line.

The inlay method alone is recommended for this pattern.

Piecing order for the inlay method (See p. 46)

1 (L1 + B3 + B5 + L3) + (B6 + B4 + L2 + L4)

2 (B1 + B7 + B2)

3 Step 1 + step 2 + H1 + H2

Appliqué the flower and leaves on to the background.

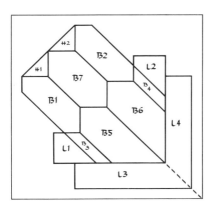

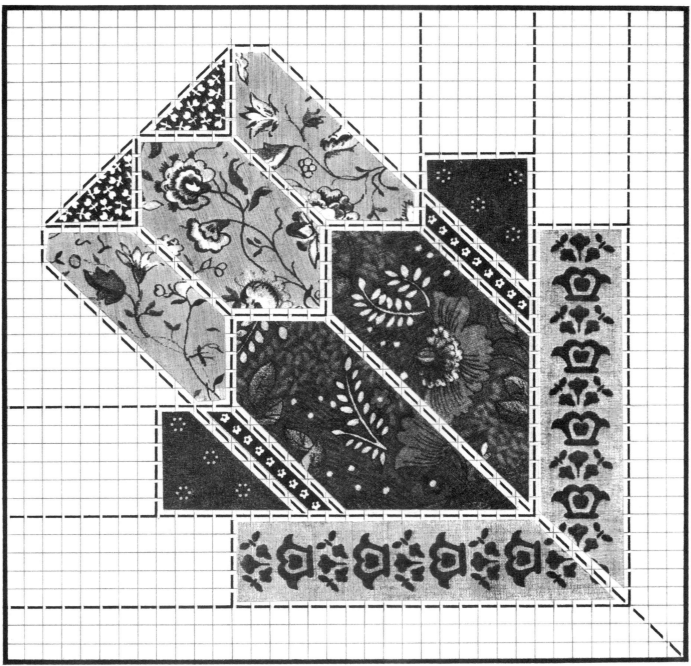

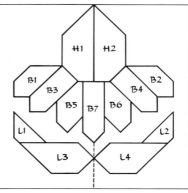

PROTEA PUNCTATA**

A small but elegant white or deep pink flower. When fully open, the bracts reveal a cone-shaped flower. The leaves are blue-green and inconspicuous.

The inlay method alone is recommended for this pattern.

Piecing order for the inlay method (See p. 46)

1 (L1 + L3) and (L4 + L2)

2 (B1 + B3 + B5 + B7) + (B6 + B4 + B2)

3 (H1 + H2) + step 2

Appliqué the flower and leaves on to the background. You can also appliqué a stem between flower and leaves.

Plate 5. *Protea punctata*. Ann Hollis (piecing). Marie Wagner (quilting).

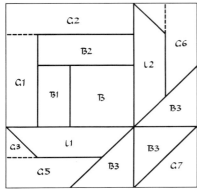

PROTEA CAFFRA*

This protea from Natal, the Eastern Cape and the Transvaal has stiff, blue-green, leathery leaves, a blackish trunk and branches, and shallow wide-open flower-heads. The bracts are deep pink with spiky white flowers.

Only the log-cabin method of piecing is recommended for this protea. As this pattern consists of just a few pattern pieces, it is better not to make the blocks larger than 27 cm. The best size for this pattern is the 18 cm square, as illustrated.

Piecing order for the log-cabin method (See p. 48)
This can be done either with or without a base fabric.

Start in the centre with B.
Then sew the other pieces in the following order: B1, B2, G1, G2, L1, L2, G3, G4, G5, G6

Piece the three triangles (B3) together according to the single-seam method.

Sew B3 as a single unit and finish with G7.

PROTEA BUD*

Most proteas have an oblong flower bud covered with light velvety bracts. The bud is usually situated at the end of a branch with leaves close by.

The log-cabin method is used for this design, either with or without a base fabric. This pattern consists of only 11 pattern pieces and must not be used for blocks larger than 18 cm x 18 cm. In fact, a smaller block of 12 cm x 12 cm is just as attractive. This pattern is also suitable for a border.

Piecing order for log-cabin method (See p. 48)
Start in the centre with B. Then sew the other pieces in the following order: G1, G2, L1, L2, G3, G4, G5, G6, G7, G8.

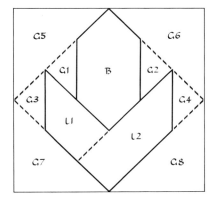

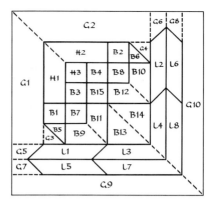

PROTEA RUBROPILOSA***

The "Wolkberg protea" has a spreading flower growing at the end of a knotty branch. The flower-heads have velvety golden-brown to rose-pink bracts. These have light yellow-brown hair on the edges.

Piecing order for the single-seam method (See p. 44)

1	G9 + (G7 + L5 + L7) + (G5 + L1 + L3)
2	Repeat for the other side.
3	(G3 + B5) + (B1 + H1) + G1
4	Repeat for the other side.
5	(B9 + B7 + B11) + B13
6	Repeat for the other side.
7	(H3 + B4) + (B3 + B15)
8	Steps 7 + 6 + 5 pieced with mitred corner.
9	(Steps 3 + 4) + step 8 pieced with mitred corner.
10	(Steps 1 + 2) + step 9 pieced with mitred corner.

Piecing order for inlay method (See p. 46)

1	(L1 + L5) + (L3 + L7)
2	Repeat for the other side.
3	(B13 + B14) + (B9 + B11 + B7) + (B10 + B12 + B8)
4	B15 + B3 + B4 + H3 + H1 + H2
5	Step 3 + (B5 + B1) + (B2 + B6) + step 1 + step 2

Appliqué the flower and leaves on to the background.

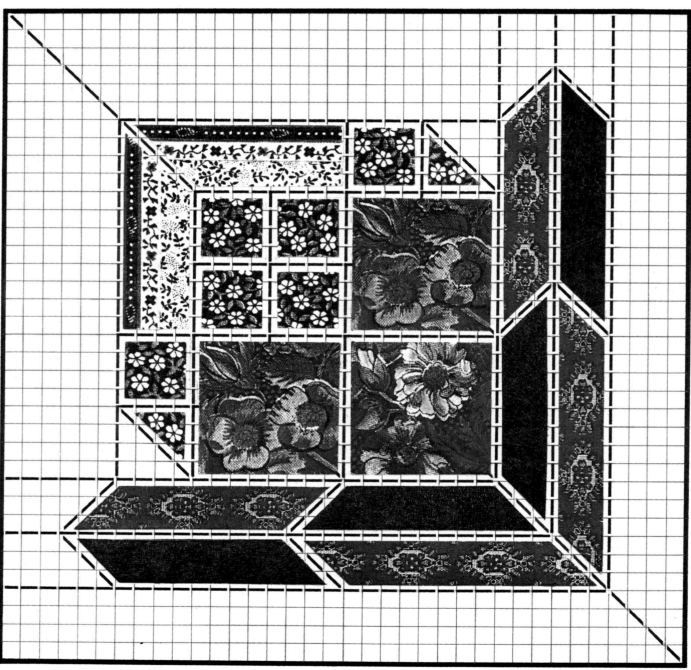

Plate 6. Fynbos (200 cm x 200 cm). Straight layout with 15 cm Log-cabin and *Protea caffra* blocks. Irene van Tonder.

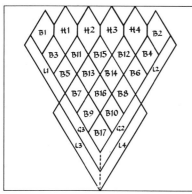

PROTEA REPENS**

This elegant V-shaped 'sugar bush' is the best-known protea in South Africa. In colonial times the nectar from the flower-head was used as a source of sweetening. The leaves are long, narrow and smooth, spatula-shaped, sometimes reaching beyond the flower-head. The sticky and shiny bracts are white to deep-red or white with pink tips. The colour of the flowers vary from milky-green to where the tips of the bracts are dark pink to red.

Please note that this protea is drawn on isometric paper, obtainable at most stationery shops. Also see p. 8 for addresses to order from.

Piecing order for inlay method (See p. 46)

1 (B17 + B9 + B10) + (B7 + B16 + B8)
2 Step 1 + (B5 + B13 + B14 + B6)
3 Step 2 + (B3 + B11 + B16 + B12 + B4)
4 Step 3 + (B1 + H1 + H2 + H3 + H4 + B2)
5 (L1 + G1 + L3) + (L2 + G2 + L4)

Appliqué the flower-head and leaves on to the background. If necessary a little stem using a bias strip folded in three can also be appliquéd on top of the leaves.

LEUCOSPERMUM BUD*

(Hexagonal pattern)

Next to the proteas, the leucospermums are the best known members of the family *Proteaceae*. They are commonly known as pincushions. As the buds open during spring the particularly colourful pincushion effect comes into being. The buds are tubular and situated at the end of stems with stubby leaves.

The piecing is done according to the inlay method only. The pattern can be reduced to make a smaller pincushion, but making it larger than the printed size is not recommended because the pattern pieces will become too clumsy.

The pattern is drawn on isometric paper.

This pattern is suitable for an overall design, a border design or in hexagonal combinations.

The hexagon shape of the flower-head need not be cut into two pattern pieces.

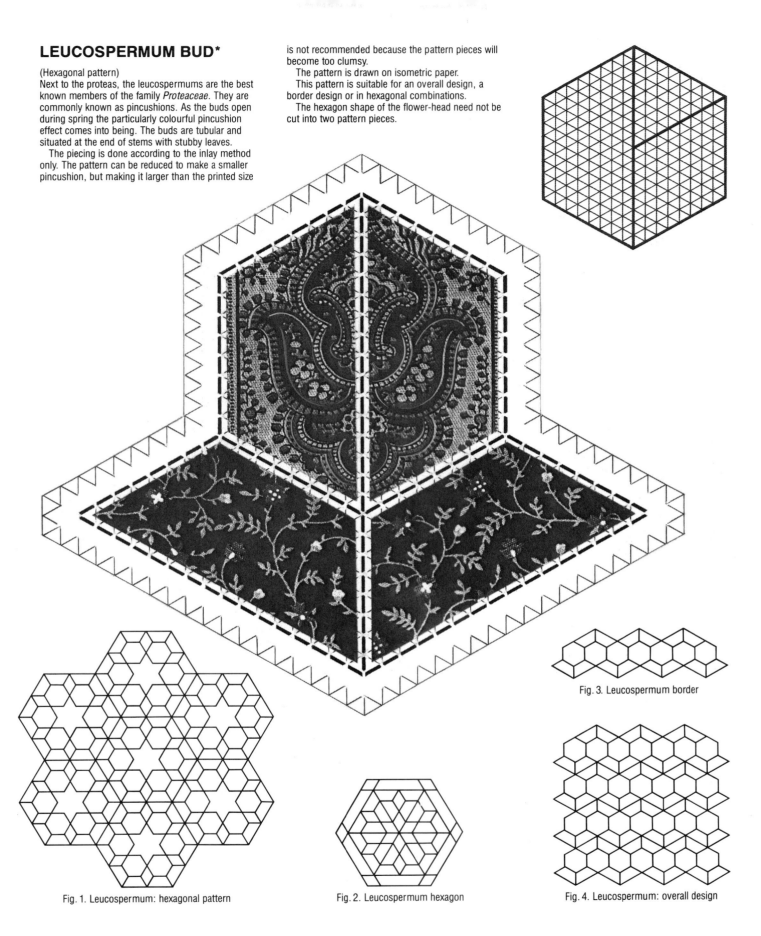

Fig. 1. Leucospermum: hexagonal pattern

Fig. 2. Leucospermum hexagon

Fig. 3. Leucospermum border

Fig. 4. Leucospermum: overall design

THE USE OF THE PATTERN BLOCK DESIGNS

As was mentioned earlier, the 18 cm x 18 cm blocks can be used the same size, one and a half times as big as, or twice the size of the pattern. All patterns should be drawn on the required size squared paper. Squared paper pads in the 5 mm or 1 cm size can be bought and all sizes ordered (addresses p. 8. Also see grids). Draw the design according to the basic pattern lines before filling in the details.

Variations on the pattern blocks

1. The position of the protea motif within the block can be changed.
Fig. 5. A slanted protea motif as it is given on the pattern page.
Fig. 6. The same protea motif moved to the bottom of the corner allowing no extra space for background fabric beyond the leaves.
Fig. 7. The same protea motif moved to the top of the corner with an extra leaf at the bottom corner.
Fig. 8. The same protea motif in a vertical position. Note that the basic block will have to be enlarged to fit this protea.

2. The basic block can be changed to form an oblong block. Please note the position of the original block demarcated by the lines in the block.
Fig. 9. A block with an upright protea motif as it is given on the pattern pages.
Fig. 10. The same protea motif with an extra leaf and extra background at the top and the bottom.
Fig. 11. Another protea motif with an extra leaf.

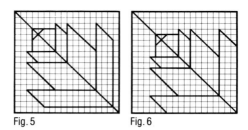

Fig. 5   Fig. 6

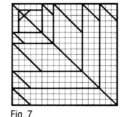

Fig. 7

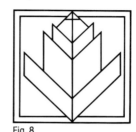

Fig. 8

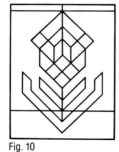 

Fig. 9

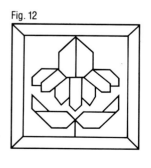

Fig. 10   Fig. 11

3. The basic block can be enlarged by:
Fig. 12. Framing an upright protea block.
Fig. 13. Framing a diagonal protea block.
Fig. 14. Using a block with a slanted protea motif, placed upright and adding four triangles to make a square block again.

4. Four blocks with slanted protea motifs can be grouped together in different ways to form a compound block.
Fig. 15. Four blocks with slanted protea motifs, moved to the corner and combined so that the leaves meet in the centre.
Fig. 16. Four blocks with slanted protea motifs moved to the corner position and made up in pairs.
Fig. 17. Four blocks with slanted protea motifs combined so that the flower motifs look toward each other and the leaves are on the outside of the block.
Fig. 18. Four blocks with vertical protea motifs partially overlapping so that only half a leaf of every block is left. Use four squares or triangles to fill in the spaces on the four corners to form a new square or new octagonal compound block.
Fig. 19. A combination of six blocks with vertical proteas (*Protea repens*).
Fig. 20. Four blocks with slanted motifs, moved to the corner position, can be combined with an extra pieced strip in the centre to form a larger compound block.
Fig. 21. Four blocks with slanted protea motifs, elongated and partially overlapping to form an oblong block.
Fig. 22. Four blocks with slanted protea motifs combined, turned diagonally with four triangles added to form a new and bigger centre.
Fig. 23. Four blocks with slanted protea motifs, forming two different pairs and overlapping in such a way that they form an oblong block.

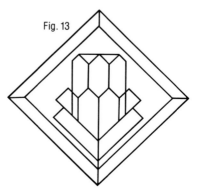

Fig. 12

Fig. 13

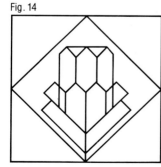

Fig. 14

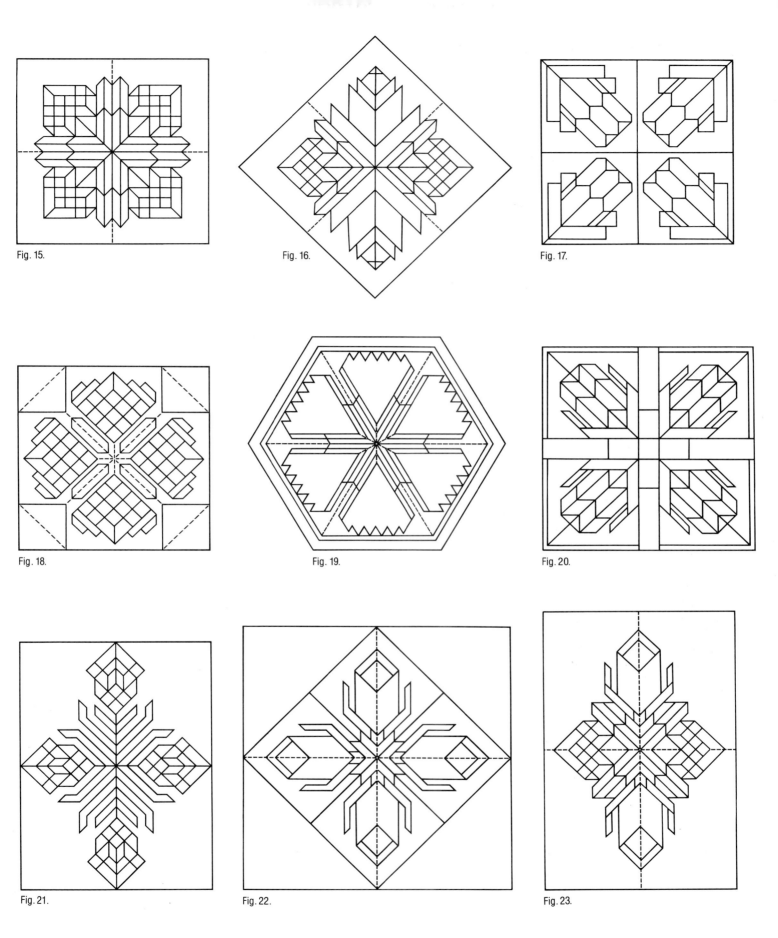

Fig. 15.

Fig. 16.

Fig. 17.

Fig. 18.

Fig. 19.

Fig. 20.

Fig. 21.

Fig. 22.

Fig. 23.

II FABRIC, THE USE OF COLOUR AND EQUIPMENT

The charm of quilting lies in the variety of fabric, different colours and shapes which are used together. These elements are responsible for the visual and emotional satisfaction derived from the unique appearance of a pieced article. The incorrect use of colour and fabric is responsible for a less than satisfactory article. The careful selection of fabric is most important in ensuring success in this art. Every quiltmaker should have the necessary knowledge of fabrics, so that she is aware of both their possibilities and limitations. An open mind towards unusual colour combinations as well as a willingness to experiment, evaluate and even radically change her mind, will all be to a quilter's advantage.

FABRIC

Theoretically, any type of fabric can be used for piecing, as long as it is pleasing and serves its purpose well. Experience soon shows that a conservative approach will be much more satisfying in the long run.

Fabrics with the same properties used in the same article will make it easier to sew, and the effects of washing on the materials will be the same. In cases where specific effects are required and a long life is not a necessity, different types of fabric may be used most effectively.

Fibre content
The most suitable fabric for piecing and quilting is cotton, with cotton mixtures of more than fifty per cent cotton an acceptable second choice.

Cotton has an advantage in that it is easy to mark, cut and piece; it folds easily and retains wrinkles, it does not fray, pieces do not slip and the needle goes through accurately. The more intricate the pattern and the smaller the pattern pieces, the more important it becomes to use pure cotton. Cotton also has flexibility and together with its natural wrinkle, gives a subtle light reflection, both sought-after properties for a good quilt.

Synthetic fabric on the other hand retains colour, but is very temperamental when it is cut and pieced. It slips in front of the scissors and needle, seams show through easily and special care must be taken when it is ironed, as the fabric may easily shrivel up or even melt.

The true nature of synthetics is that they are wrinkle-resistant, with the result that they easily look rather like plastic. Some cottons are treated to obtain all the properties of the synthetics, and these should be avoided. Synthetics are also responsible for a build-up of static electricity and will soil easily. Over a period, a synthetic batting will also be responsible for fibre migration, showing little beards of batting on the right side of the fabric.

Weight
Thick and heavy fabrics are difficult to sew and seams are often uneven. Corners are matched with difficulty. Seams also tend not to stay flat when pressed.

Lightweight fabrics are easy to use and make it relatively simple to piece and quilt accurately. No extra weight is added to the quilt. Lightness is much sought after in a comfortable quilt, especially in a bed quilt.

Weave
Fabrics with an even, plain weave are preferable to fancy weaves and knitted fabrics because piecing can be done accurately and the quilting stitches look neatest and show up best on plain fabrics. Twill and satin weaves form a diagonal line, and though these fabrics can be soft, they stretch when they are pieced and the quilting stitch disappears behind the threads. Pile fabrics are also difficult to sew and should be avoided. Sail cloth is too thick and heavy.

The closeness of the weave will eventually influence the ease and speed with which you can execute the quilting. The fabrics you choose should not hamper the piecing and quilting process.

Needle test
It is advisable to test selected fabrics with a needle to ensure that the sewing process will start smoothly. Hold a single piece of fabric tightly between the fingers of your left hand, take a needle in your right and punch the needle quickly through the fabric. If the needle penetrates the fabric easily end securely, without leaving a hole in the fabric and without clinging to the fabric or shifting, it should be acceptable.

Preparing fabric for quilting
Except for 100 per cent synthetic batting, all fabrics to be used for quilts which will eventually require cleaning should be preshrunk. This is to ensure that the fabric will not shrink afterwards, that colour does not run and also to get rid of superfluous starch. Soak light and dark fabrics separately in hot water at 40 degrees Celsius. Pre-test for colour fastness. If the colour should run, soak in

vinegar or salt water (125 ml vinegar or 10 ml salt in 2 litres of water) for 10 minutes. Rinse in clean water and make sure no further colour bleeding takes place. This is especially necessary for prints. Always use fabric softener in the final rinsing water to decrease static electricity.

THE USE OF COLOUR

The colour and print on fabric
The possibilities for fabric combinations for quilts are endless and every quilter will combine fabrics to suit her own mood and personality to make original combinations.

A quilt should be alive regardless of whether four or forty fabrics have been used together. It only makes sense to cut up fabric if the new combination is more pleasing and exciting than the original fabric. Piecing fabric together requires continuous evaluation and adaptation as the work proceeds.

In most cases the texture of the fabric, as well as the design, will dictate your choice. An open mind to colour combinations and a willingness to make adjustments are the essence of original quilting design and pleasure.

Solids and prints can be used equally successfully for pieced quilts. Solids look bold and dramatic while prints usually look softer, giving an antique impression. Prints and solids used together are more cottage-like. Prints also give the illusion of texture. To change texture use prints with different-sized motifs, both small and large prints, overall and isolated motifs.

Light and dark fabrics should be combined in a quilt, unless a very subtle effect is desired. The dark fabric ensures that pattern pieces are linked visually and the lighter fabrics provide the space for pattern pieces to stand out clearly. The illusion of depth comes from using light, medium and dark-coloured fabrics together. In most cases the inclusion of a few prints with black guarantees success.

To ensure continuinty in a quilt, some fabric pieces should be repeated. For instance, use the same fabric in the centre as well as along the borders. Using a darker centre and repeating it on the edges is often most successful.

Colouring the fabric
The use of colouring agents and textile dyes to create new colours for cotton fabrics is fast becoming popular. The most successful method is to dye fabrics in a strong solution of water and tea or filter coffee. Prepare the fabric as described on p. 26. Bring the solution to the boil in a saucepan and let the damp fabric simmer in it for about 20 minutes. Remove the fabric, place it in a solution of boiling water and vinegar (125 ml vinegar to 2 litres of water) and leave to cool. Then wash the fabric thoroughly to ensure that it is colour-fast.

A fabric collection
A nine-block fabric grid is recommended for the beginner to guide her to a successful collection of fabric pieces. If all spaces in the grid are filled with different fabrics, an article produced will surely look good. The fabrics need not necessarily be of the same colour range, but should not jar. Small, medium and large prints should be incorporated as well as light, medium and dark coloured fabrics. Solids and border prints can then be added to the fabric grid for more variety.

Explaining a fabric collection:

Small prints, especially in tones of one or two colours, are exceptionally suitable for smaller pattern pieces. The closeness of the print and the colour of the background will determine whether the print has a light, medium or dark value. These fabrics, especially when colour combinations are subtle, are excellent as the background.

Medium prints give a pleasing overall effect and usually have more colours and shadings than small prints. These fabrics are especially effective when used for medium-sized pattern pieces and can also be used as background. In some

cases they are printed in such a way that motifs can be placed to fit the centre of the pattern pieces. If these prints look busy they should not be used on large pattern pieces.

Large prints, especially those with flower or paisley motifs printed as single motifs or continuous lines, look good placed symmetrically in the protea designs as centre pieces. They can also be used as specific oblong or square pattern pieces. Always consider the natural growth of the flower to decide the correct direction of these types of prints. In cases where a very large fabric print is available it can be used as an unpieced pattern block.

Fabrics with regular border prints or stripes are ideally suited for borders, sashes and oblong pattern pieces and, in some cases, as the top piece of the protea head. In this case they must be pieced in such a way as to form a mitred corner (see *Protea cynaroides,* p. 12). These fabrics are sometimes available as piece goods or already cut as single border strips. Use them for bordering quilts. If printed symmetrically, border prints can also be used in pattern pieces

(see *Protea punctata,* p. 16, and *Protea neriifolia,* p. 13).

Background fabrics can be solids or large or small prints, dark or light, bright or dull. The whole background can be of the same fabric, though different background fabrics can make a quilt look more interesting. The important aspect is that the pieced protea must stand out against the background. Geometric fabrics are not suitable for backgrounds unless they are very cleverly used. They usually interfere with the more subtle lines of the piecing. Busy prints and prints with a big contrast are not suitable for the background.

Fabrics to be avoided
Theoretically, any fabric can be used for piecing, but on the other hand it is advisable not to use the following types when you are starting to collect materials for the background: large geometric prints which interfere with piecing lines and look confusing; one-way designs; fabric with a directional sheen (it requires a lot more special care when pieced to ensure that it is symmetrical and gives the idea of radiating from the centre outwards); too much colour contrast or too many colours (as it appears grey from a distance and will not blend in when viewed close up); and fabric with a white background which is difficult to match, has too much contrast and shows dirt easily. Do not include busy prints in the fabric background because they are visually disturbing and look untidy when pieced in a quilt. Do not attempt to have all fabrics in the same size print or try to get colours to match accurately.

Fabrics for borders
Most quilts will look best with a medium or dark border, preferably of a fabric used in the piecing. A light border can easily look undefined and pieces will tend to "move out" of the quilt. There are exceptions to this rule, so it is advisable not to decide finally about the border before the piecing is finished and the quilt can be pinned up against a board or curtain and evaluated from a distance.

Fabrics for a quilt back
An important consideration for the back of a quilt is that it must be practical, not too tightly woven and lightweight, so as not to impede the quilting process. It must be aesthetically pleasing and should match the quilt-top. Any finely woven 100 per cent cotton small print or solid is suitable. Left-over fabric from the top can easily be pieced and used for the backing, in which case it should be pieced symmetrically. Care must be taken not to have too many seams because it will make the quilting difficult. Get rid of all selvedges. Open the seams after sewing and press them flat. Permanently pressed sheeting should not be used for backing because the thread count is too high, making it too tightly woven, too thick and heavy and impenetrable by the average quilter.

Batting
The batting is the layer between the quilt-top and the back. It gives body to the quilt and also serves as an isolation in cases where the quilt is used as a blanket, and it makes the quilting stitches show as indents. Traditionally, tufted cotton or wool were used so quilting lines had to be close together to prevent the fibres from forming lumps.

Today, batting is available in a variety of thicknesses, qualities, softness and fibre mixtures. Usually the mass per square unit is a reasonable indication of the volume and thickness. The 100 per cent synthetic battings are usually bonded to prevent the fibres from moving when being washed. This property allows the quilter to choose the amount of quilting and the density of quilting from the decorative point of view and not so much because of the need for it. Batting should be chosen on the thickness, the volume, the weight and its inherent ability to be pliable and soft.

Types of batting
1
Double thickness extra loft 800-1 000 g/m² is suitable for sleeping bags and knotted quilts made commercially.
2
Thick extra loft batting 600 g/m² is also suitable for sleeping bags, knotted and

Plate 7. Leucospermum rainbow (94 cm x 120 cm, with a 13 cm binding strip). June Kruger.

puffed quilts. This can be used for hand quilting but will take time and is difficult to sew. The non-quilted area will be very puffed but it will be impossible to work tiny quilting stitches.

3

The in-between thicknesses, 100-400 g/m², are most suitable for hand quilting, and can also be used for machine quilting at home, with the necessary accessories. This batting is less than 2 cm thick and on the outside looks like a thick blanket, but pressed together, is rather thin.

4

Fleece or thin batting looks like puffed felt, but is very thin and soft. It is suitable for table centrepieces, cushions and small wall hangings where too much dimension is not necessary. This batting mixed with cotton is especially suitable for lightweight quilts and apparel.

5

Needlepunch batting is much heavier and stiffer than fleece, though it also can be used for cushions, table centrepieces and even wall hangings. However, the puffed areas will be rather flat and the quilt will lose some dimension.

6

Woven cotton flannel or flannelette can also be used for flat quilting. It is not advisable to split a thick batting to use as a quilt batting because the bonded area is only on one side and the fibres will migrate through the fabric after some wear.

Choice of fabric for protea blocks
The pleasure of any textile art lies in a rich and colourful variety of fabric combinations. Don't spoil this part of the process by too many preconceived ideas of colour combinations. Sometimes it might just be a specific fabric that sets the spark for a most extraordinary combination, or the inspiration may come from a painting, carpet or curtaining in a room. The important aspect to remember is that proteas need not be realistic in colour; what is essential is that the protea should stand out against its background.

For the beginner, choosing the background might be a good starting point. It can be light or dark, printed or solid fabric. Of course, the background fabric should not necessarily be the same throughout the quilt. Alternating background fabric for overall block layouts and variegated backgrounds for medallion layouts are most interesting — and necessary! Choosing the fabric for a specific protea is always done on a background because the flower must be offset against the background. If, by any chance, the flower melts into the background, which can easily happen on the edge of the flower-head, it can be offset by a darker narrow borderprint, appliquéd at this edge.

It is possible to make the whole flower in only one fabric; or two fabrics with the flower-head in one colour and the leaves in a second; or with three fabrics with the flower-head, leaves and bracts showing up against each other. Within these divisions, more fabrics can be added.

Prints with defined motifs are especially suitable for use in specific patterns.

Evaluate the choice of fabric
See to it that all fabrics used in an article are suitable for their purpose. The entire protea motif — including leaves, bracts and head must stand out against the background. Include dark, medium and light fabrics to ensure liveliness and good balance. Every piece of fabric must come to life in the place where it is used.

Amount of fabric
There are no set rules on how to use fabrics, so it is impossible to state specific material requirements for a particular pattern, unless a pattern is copied exactly. The whole quilt must be seen as a continuous creative process allowing for several changes of mind and consequently of fabric requirements.

The total amount of fabric you need for a quilt-top is usually one-and-a-half times to twice as much as needed for the total area to be covered.

For border prints allow enough material to frame the whole quilt. It is advisable to repeat the same border print. The material required for specific border prints will depend on the number of repeats and the area to be covered.

Buy more fabric than the estimated amount needed — or team up with a friend who also collects fabrics. Leftovers can always be used, but running short can be most frustrating.

EQUIPMENT

Patchwork and quilting can be mastered with ordinary sewing tools, though a few special items will be worth their cost because they ease some time-consuming tasks and thus ensure an enjoyable creative experience.

The correct *needle* for a specific task ensures regular stitch lengths and fast work speed. The higher the number, the finer the needle, and the easier it is to make fine, regular stitches. For tacking, use a Sharps no. 7 or 8. For piecing and quilting, only the "between" in no. 8, 9, 10 and even 12 will ensure that the correct method of sewing can be achieved.

Long, thin, rust-free *tailor's pins* are essential. You can also buy special quilter's pins for specific purposes.

Three pairs of *scissors* are a must: a long-bladed pair which can cut accurately through six layers of fabric, a long-bladed pair for paper and a short, lightweight pair for snipping.

A *rotary cutter* with *cutting pad* and a set of 60 cm *perspex strips* are necessary for cutting fabric strips. The cutter and pad are available at hardware, graphic art and sewing shops. Perspex strips can usually be cut to fit your requirements (3; 5; 7,5 and 10 cm in width) wherever you buy them. These three items ensure straight cutting lines and eliminates cutting with a pair of scissors to a large extent.

You will also need a *cutting knife* or blade for cutting paper and pattern templates.

100 per cent mercerized cotton thread is recommended. Cotton polyester thread is the second choice. Do not use synthetic thread as this cuts the cotton fabric. For basting use no. 120; for piecing and quilting no. 30 double mercerized cotton thread run through beeswax, or quilting thread especially made for this purpose.

If only mercerized thread is available, run it through beeswax before using it.

A single-thread cotton floss, run through beeswax, usually available in a large variety of colours, is also suitable for quilting. Choose the colour of the thread to match the largest area of the quilt-top. For piecing, match the lighter colour of the pieces and for quilting use the same colour as the fabric, or somewhat darker than the lightest colour. Or you can use different colours to match every pattern piece.

The shadow effect formed by the indent of the quilting stitch will be sharpened if a darker thread is used.

Thread the needle from the bobbin without cutting the thread (Fig. 24).

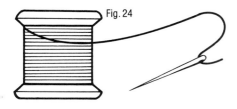
Fig. 24

Make a neat knot by winding the thread around the needle and pulling the needle through (Fig. 25).

Fig. 25

Thimbles are chosen to fit the individual's finger size and shape, one for the middle finger of the right hand to give the leverage for sewing and pushing the needle through the fabric, and one for the forefinger of the left hand to prevent the finger tip being pricked. Special thimbles are available, for example, one with a little gap to leave the nail open and with an edge preventing the needle slipping from the thimble. Leather thimbles with a small metal insert are especially suitable. Other leather and metal finger protectors especially for quilting are also available.

Beeswax is commercially available. All cotton thread which is not marked as "quilting thread" should be drawn through beeswax twice. This reinforces the thread and lessens tangling. The excess wax should be removed by

drawing it through the finger-nails before it is cut from the reel, or before you thread the needle.

Fabric markers are essential and must be kept sharpened. To mark stitching lines and corresponding corners, use a light pencil (such as a 2H graphite pencil) for light fabrics, and for dark fabrics use a soft graphite pencil (such as a 2B), a white drawing pencil or a silver graphite pencil. A charcoal art pencil is also suitable.

Tailor's chalk and pencils can be used. A very fine felt-tipped pen should be used *only* to mark cutting lines effectively on a dark fabric. Magic markers are not recommended, as the ink might easily bleed and ruin the fabric.

A variety of *rulers* are useful: an ordinary plastic ruler, 30-40 cm long, for regular drawings (grading must be on the bottom); a 15 cm ruler (with 1 mm markings) for templates; a 6 mm x 6 mm x 20 cm *plastic rod* to mark seam allowances (Quilter's quarter); and a set of transparent perspex strips, 3 mm thick and 60 cm long, in widths 3; 5; 7,5 and 10 cm, to be used as cutting guides for fabric strips.

A metal *sewing gauge* with a sliding marker is useful to measure 6 mm seam allowances, to draw circles and to measure widths.

A *french curve* or compass or a swivel stencil is recommended to mark and measure curved designs.

An *iron with pressing cloth and cotton towelling pressing area* are essential. Make sure that the iron is clean; control the temperature of the iron and always press on the wrong side with the cloth — even if a steam iron is used. When stitching by machine, frequent pressing is necessary. When sewing by hand, only fingerpress the seams and don't use the iron until a whole unit is finished. Be careful not to destroy the fabric texture by ironing too often and at too high a temperature.

Squared paper is the most reliable aid to ensure accuracy. Check all squared paper with a measuring apparatus to make sure the squares are true, for instance squared paper marked in in 5 mm squares for rectangular and tri-

angular designs, and isometric paper for hexagonal designs. (Calculation and isometric pads are available in stationery shops, or could be ordered from the addresses on p. 8 in 5 mm, 7,5 mm or 1 cm squares for 18, 27 and 36 cm pattern blocks.)

Glue and *template cardboard* or *transparent plastic* are necessary for making templates. The cardboard must be index-card weight.

Frames to be used for the quilting process are recommended for all articles except the very small ones. There are several frame types to choose from: A special round or oval *quilting hoop*, about 60 cm in diameter, is available. The advantage of the hoop is that it can be easily manipulated and is simple to move around, so that quilting can be resumed almost anywhere.

Embroidery frames with two roller and two straining beams are suitable for quilting cushions and small wall units. A frame like this can easily be made at home. Take four beams, 70 cm long, 5 cm wide and 1 cm thick. Make a slit lengthwise through both ends of each beam. Secure two of the beams on top of the other two at a right angle by using four sets of wing nuts and bolts. Shift the beams to form the desired size square. For larger quilts two of the beams must be substituted for longer beams.

Quilting frames for larger articles such as bed quilts are commercially available but can also be made at home. Use firm, thick planks. The two roller beams must be 20-30 cm longer than the shorter sides of the quilt. The straining beam can be from 70 cm to the length required. Instead of bolts and wing nuts, four ordinary "G" clamps available from hardware stores can be used to hold the planks in position. A big frame like this can be supported on trestles, or on a table and chair back or windowsill, or whatever is available in the home. To pack it away, it can be hung or put up straight against the wall, or even hoisted to the ceiling.

A quilt top consists of a collection of blocks, strips of fabric and frames with or without piecing, which can be laid out in several ways. The pattern blocks for the protea, how they are drawn, changed and combined is discussed in the Introduction.

Now we set out the layout of these blocks for a variety of articles with special reference to bed quilts.

SIZE

The sizes of quilts vary from small wall quilts to large bed quilts, 3 m x 3 m, to enormous quilts which cover metres and metres of wall space in porches and halls. The size of individual pieces depends on the eventual use.

For a bed quilt, the size and height of the mattress, the height of the bed and individual preferences are important. Decide, prior to designing, whether night frills are going to be used, whether cushions are going to be placed on top or under the quilt and whether the quilt is going to be tucked in at the bottom end of the bed or not. (A quilt is preferably not tucked in under a mattress.) A small, square or oblong quilt can be just thrown over a bed.

It is important to know where wall quilts are eventually going to hang. The quilts can fit into a niche or be hung on a wall with enough surrounding space to show the quilt off to its fullest advantage.

Provision must be made for 2-4 per cent and sometimes even up to 8 per cent shrinkage of the quilt during the quilting process. Exactly how much shrinkage will take place, will depend on the thickness of the batting and the closeness of the quilting stitch.

Pattern blocks for the proteas are shown as 18 cm x 18 cm. It is recommended that all articles should be made with blocks 18 cm, 27 cm or 36 cm square:

☐ Single blocks, 18 cm x 18 cm are suitable for a bell pull.
☐ A combination block which forms a 36 cm square with a 4-6 cm frame is suitable for a cushion, shopping bag or a small wall hanging.
☐ Single blocks, especially those with few pattern pieces, are especially suitable for border designs.
☐ A combination block with 27 cm square or 36 cm square blocks is suitable for a table centrepiece, a cover for a continental cushion, or for a wall hanging. The larger combination is also suitable for the centre of a medallion quilt.
☐ Thirty-six single blocks, 27 cm or 36 cm squares, are enough for a bed quilt, if some unpieced blocks and fabric borders are included.
☐ A single block, 27 cm square or elongated, is big enough for a wall quilt or a small cushion.

THE LAYOUT OF A QUILT

The way in which pattern blocks are put together to form an overall effect is known as the layout. There are four basic layouts: the strip layout; the block layout which can be either a straight layout (Fig. 26) or a diagonal layout (Fig. 27); the medallion layout (Fig. 28), which consists of a straight or diagonal centre with borders and blocks framing it; and an overall-layout. A quilt is usually designed and assembled according to one or a combination of these layouts.

Variations of these basic layouts are obtained by using sashes (strips of fabric) between blocks (Fig. 29), or purposely not assembling blocks in straight lines, (Fig. 30) or by making combinations of these layouts (Fig. 31). In addition, block sizes can vary in the same article.

Further variety is gained by using fabric in an original and interesting way, especially when border prints are included.

A quilt can be elongated by using more blocks in the length, by changing the block patterns into oblong blocks, or by including more or perhaps wider borders in the length.

SCALE AND PLANNING OF THE QUILT

Planning according to scale will be easier if you follow this method:
☐ Choose the scale you are going to use before you begin drawing — for example, 1 cm = 18 cm. Use the same scale throughout the project.
☐ Draw the outside measurements of the article on the squared paper according to the set scale. For a standard quilt it would be approximately 250 cm x 250 cm, with either 27 cm or 36 cm square blocks.
☐ Draw 30 blocks to scale on squared paper.
☐ Complete these blocks, roughly indicating either a vertical or slanted protea, or an empty block.
☐ Draw more blocks, some square,

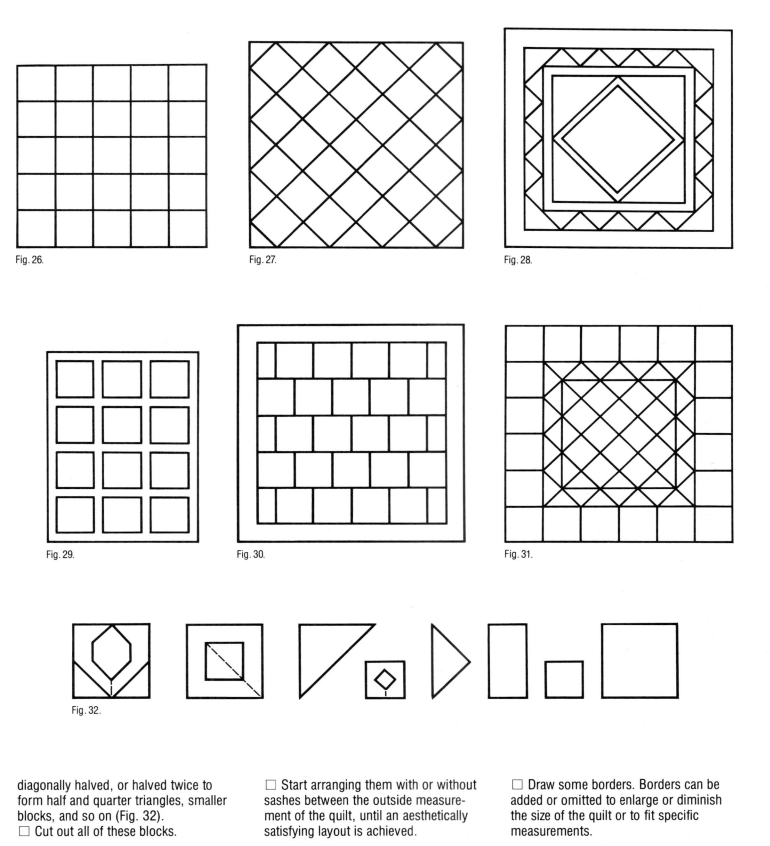

Fig. 26.

Fig. 27.

Fig. 28.

Fig. 29.

Fig. 30.

Fig. 31.

Fig. 32.

diagonally halved, or halved twice to form half and quarter triangles, smaller blocks, and so on (Fig. 32).
☐ Cut out all of these blocks.

☐ Start arranging them with or without sashes between the outside measurement of the quilt, until an aesthetically satisfying layout is achieved.

☐ Draw some borders. Borders can be added or omitted to enlarge or diminish the size of the quilt or to fit specific measurements.

Plate 8. Swing-glass (234 cm x 198 cm). Medallion layout with inlay method. Maretha Fourie (piecing and quilting). Marie Wagner (quilting).

Examples of quilt layouts

☐ Fig. 33. *Straight layout*, consisting of eight slanted protea blocks, eight empty blocks with motif quilting, pieced and unpieced sashes and a border.
Size: 207 cm x 207 cm, with 36 single blocks and 9 cm sashes.

☐ Fig. 34. *Straight layout* with five combined squares with slanted protea blocks, four combined squares with vertical protea blocks and a border.
Size: 252 cm x 252 cm, with 36 cm blocks.

☐ Fig 35. *Diagonal layout* with slanted protea blocks, ten empty blocks for motif quilting, fourteen half-size triangles, four quarter block size triangles and a border.
Size: 280 cm x 240 cm, with 36 cm blocks.

☐ Fig. 36. *Diagonal layout* with eight vertical protea blocks, twelve slanted protea blocks, five empty blocks for motif quilting and twelve half-size triangles. (Please note the straight grain on the triangles.)
Size: 234 cm x 234 cm, with 36 cm blocks.

☐ Fig. 37. *Diagonal layout* with five combined squares with four slanted proteas, with sashes, triangles and a frame. (Please note the lengthwise and crosswise grain arrows on the triangles.)
Size: 270 cm x 270 cm, with 36 cm blocks.

☐ Fig. 38. *Diagonal layout* with eight slanted protea blocks, four vertical protea blocks and filled in with half-size blocks and triangles.
Size: 252 cm x 252 cm with 36 cm blocks.

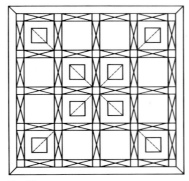

Fig. 33.

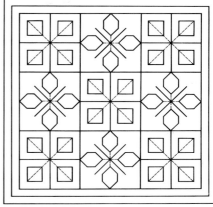

Fig. 34.

Fig. 35.

Fig. 36.

Fig. 37.

Fig. 38.

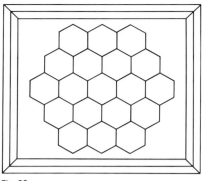

Fig. 39

Fig. 40

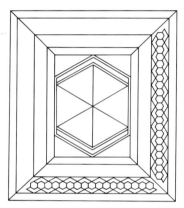

Fig. 41

Fig. 42

Fig. 43

Fig. 44

☐ Fig. 39. *Overall layout* with 19 leucospermum hexagons combined in such a way that they form the middle of the quilt.

Size: 238 cm x 207 cm, with hexagonal blocks as indicated by pattern on p. 23.

☐ Fig. 40. *Medallion layout* with one combined square with slanted protea blocks, changed to a diagonal position in the centre, with sashes and 36 protea buds (quarter-size blocks) with empty blocks and triangles used as a border.

Size: 220 cm x 220 cm, with 36 cm blocks.

☐ Fig. 41. *Medallion layout* with six *Protea repens* blocks in the centre and a border with leucospermum buds.

Size: 240 cm x 200 cm, with 36 cm blocks.

☐ Fig. 42. *Combination layout* with one combined square diagonally placed with four slanted protea blocks, four vertical protea blocks, four empty blocks for motif quilting, twelve triangles (quarter-size blocks) and a border with four empty quarter-size blocks on the corners.

Size: 180 cm x 252 cm, with 36 cm blocks.

☐ Fig. 43. *Medallion layout* with one combined oblong with vertical protea blocks in the centre, with sashes, with 26 protea buds, quarter-size blocks and a border.

Size: 240 cm x 180 cm, with 36 cm blocks and 18 cm buds.

☐ Fig. 44. *Medallion layout* with one combined oblong with diagonally cut corners made up of vertical protea blocks, with sashes and triangles, with four slanted protea blocks (27 cm blocks), with frames and four empty quarter-size blocks in the corners.

Size: 198 cm x 234 cm with 36 cm and 27 cm centre blocks.

36

FRAMING THE QUILT TOP
(See Fig. 45)

A quilt top usually consists of pieced and unpieced blocks, sometimes sashes between blocks, and a final border which frames the quilt. Sashes and borders vary in width and can be very plain, for example just a strip of fabric, or they can be decorative with intricate piecing of blocks, triangles and strips of fabric. Border prints are exceptionally useful for framing.

The planning of borders should be done at the start of the designing stage. It is advisable to work with units of the block sizes, though wider blocks can easily be used. A final decision on the borders can only be made after the quilt is complete and is being evaluated.

Here are a few hints on planning the border of a quilt.

☐ The border around the quilt must define the quilt and at the same time acentuate the central design. The border usually looks best if it is in dark or medium colours and forms a continuous line around the quilt.

☐ The border must form a unit with the quilt top. This is achieved by avoiding new colours, shapes and lines. Rather repeat some of the fabrics used in the centre, or repeat the same shapes or lines or theme.

☐ The border must look well balanced, so make sure the corners are symmetrical. If a mirror image is to be obtained, the pattern must be reversed from the middle of the border.

☐ Large oblong pieces and long border strips should be cut on the lengthwise grain of the fabric, unless special pattern effects are to be achieved. If a special effect can only be achieved by cutting on the bias, sew a stay stitch on the seam line.

☐ If the corner of the quilt top must be cut away diagonally to fit a bed more perfectly, the frame must still go around the corner.

☐ If borders have not been cut long enough and piecing is necessary, it must be done in the centre of the side, or symmetrically at two places, or the seam must correspond with the seam on the inside of the quilt layout.

Fig. 45

☐ Arrows suggest the recommended lengthwise or crosswise grain.
☐ Remember to add seam allowances.

Sashes and borders
When piecing strips of fabric for sashes and borders, stitch them to the centrepiece with continuous stitching. Treat a corner by overlapping it, thus forming a straight corner with a single piece of fabric, or piece on a corner with an extra square. A corner can also be mitred. The length or width of a border strip will depend on the individual articles. Allow for seams.

Follow the same rules for cushions, wall quilts or bed covers (even medallion quilts are pieced in this way).

1. The straight corner (Fig. 46)
Method:
☐ Mark the seam lines and the corner dots of the article accurately on the wrong side.
☐ Cut two opposite border strips the same length as the article and sew on two opposite sides of the article. Press

seams together towards the darker fabric.
☐ Cut the other two border strips the same length as the article *plus* twice the width of the border.
☐ Sew these two strips on the remaining sides of the article to form an overlapping straight corner (Fig. 47).

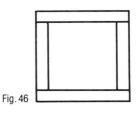

Fig. 46

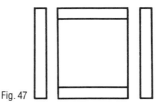

Fig. 47

☐ If squares are to be pieced in the corners, this must be done in exactly the

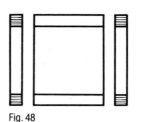 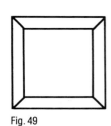 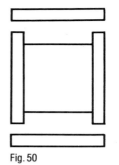 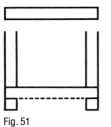 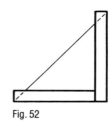

Fig. 48   Fig. 49   Fig. 50   Fig. 51   Fig. 52

same way except that all four borders are cut the same length and the four squares are added on to the two opposite borders, being sewn on last (Fig. 48).

2. *The mitred corner* (Fig. 49)
The mitred corner with its diagonal corner-line is especially suitable when obviously diagonal lines exist in the pieced areas.
In most cases this corner looks stunning.
Method:
□ Mark opposite sides and the corners of the article accurately.

□ Cut all four border strips twice their width larger than the seam they should match.
□ Sew two opposite border strips from corner dot to corner dot exactly (Fig. 50), so that they extend past the dots.
□ Then sew the other two border strips exactly from corner dot to corner dot (Fig. 51).
□ Press the seam allowances together, preferably towards the darker fabric.
□ Fold the whole article diagonally, keeping right sides together, so as to

place the border strips on top of each other.
□ Use the 60 cm plastic strip and put it straight with the diagonal line extending over the border strips. Mark this diagonal line on the border (Fig. 52).
□ Sew the border strips together on the line, sewing from the edge of the border towards the marked dot on the corner. Ensure that the corner is perfect, and trim.
□ Press the seems of the corner open.
Never cut the border diagonally before it is pieced, because it will stretch while sewing.

Plate 9. *Left:* Centre-piece of a wall quilt, Proteas, with straight layout (36 and 18 cm blocks). Maretha Fourie and others. *Right:* Centre-piece of a wall quilt. Loretta Rheeler.

Fig. 53. Straight layout with 5 combined squares; *Protea cynaroides* in the centre and *Protea rubropilosa* in the corners. Size: 288 cm x 288 cm; 36 cm blocks

Fig. 54. Diagonal layout with one combined square (*Protea barbigera*) in the centre, and 52 *Protea caffra* blocks making up the border. Cut the dotted fabric in blocks as well to contribute to the diagonal effect. Size: 276 cm x 228 cm; 36 cm blocks. The *Protea caffra* blocks are 18 cm square

Fig. 55. Medallion quilt with only one combined oblong in the centre and 36 protea buds with additional borders and triangles. *Protea lacticolor* has been used as the centre design. Size: 234 cm x 198 cm; 36 cm blocks in the centre and 18 cm blocks for the protea bud designs

Fig. 56. Cushion: 45 cm x 45 cm; 18 cm blocks

Fig. 57. Table centre-piece:
100 cm x 72 cm; 27 cm blocks

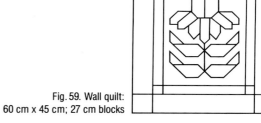

Fig. 59. Wall quilt:
60 cm x 45 cm; 27 cm blocks

Fig. 58. Table centre-piece:
81 cm x 81 cm; 27 cm blocks

Fig. 60. Wall quilt:
120 cm x 30 cm; 18 cm blocks

Fig. 61. Wall quilt: 126 cm x 126 cm; 27 cm blocks

Plate 10. Protea Brillianté (254 cm x 254 cm). Diagonal layout with 21 cm *Protea caffra* blocks. Maretha Fourie and others.

IV PIECING

To turn the pattern blocks into decorative fabric blocks, first draw the design to scale on squared paper, made up of 5 mm squares for the 18 cm block size, 7,5 mm squares for 27 cm and 1 cm squares for 36 cm blocks. The grids printed in the front and back of the book may be photocopied or traced to obtain a working copy. Drawings can be done in pencil (2B), so that it is easily correctible. The working copy is used to make templates, etc.

The block size must be suitable for the article, though sizes can be chosen at random. The printed size, one-and-a-half times printed size or twice printed size are realistic for most patterns, unless otherwise specified. *Protea caffra* and the protea bud have too few pattern pieces for large blocks, and should not be bigger than a 24 cm block. The leuco-spermum pattern, too, should not be made any larger than the printed size. All other blocks can be doubled.

MAKING TEMPLATES

As was said in the Introduction all block patterns must be redrawn by first sketch-ing the outlines and halving the lines to locate the central point. Now draw in different pattern pieces, and identify each piece by a symbol and a number.

Proceed as follows:
☐ Make a photocopy of the drawing or trace it on to another sheet of paper. Fill in the symbols for every pattern piece on both copies.
☐ If only one protea block is going to be made, cut up this paper copy into templates.

☐ If more than one protea is going to be made from the same pattern, this copy should be glued on to cardboard (index-card thickness) and every pattern cut out with a cutting knife. (A piece of sand-paper or masking tape must be pasted on to the back of every pattern template to prevent the pattern shifting off the fabric.)
☐ Note that there are no seam allowances.

CUTTING OUT FABRIC PIECES

☐ Lay the individual templates on the wrong side of the chosen fabric.
☐ See that the thread runs in the same direction as the lines on the squared paper, unless special design effects are required.
☐ Draw the stitching line around every template and mark the turning point at every corner with a dot. Accuracy is most important at this point, and can be obtained by using a very sharp pencil and a ruler.
☐ Draw the 6 mm seam allowance around the template on the fabric, using the Quilter's quarter.
☐ Cut out every pattern piece in sequence from the bottom of the flower to the top, and then the leaves. Lay the pieces on the background fabric immediately and continually evaluate the choice of fabric. Remember that a small piece of fabric may look very different from the original piece, and that the fabric next to it may also influence the visual effect. If the background is to be pieced, it must also be cut out. Other-wise only the flower motif should be cut out and the background cut into a block size.

☐ Make sure at this stage that the protea motif stands out clearly against the background fabrics.
☐ Pin every pattern piece in position on a piece of fabric, right side up. This will prevent a mix-up. Next, piece the protea according to one of the following three methods: the single-seam method, the inlay method and the folding-over method. Use the recommended method where possible.

PIECING

1. The single-seam method (block or American block method)
Fabric pieces are hand-sewn with the right sides together using small running stitches or machine-sewn with a single seam. The success of this method depends largely on whether the pieces were cut and marked accurately, as seams must fit perfectly. The sequence in which the fabric pieces are stitched together is also important.

Method:
☐ Place two pieces, right sides together, so that seam allowances match. Pin the marked corners exactly with two pins perpendicularly on the seamline.
☐ Start the thread with a knot and a back-stitch exactly on the marked dot (Fig. 62). Never work in the seam allowance.
☐ Stitch the two seams together, keeping to the marked stitching line. Use a small running stitch or a piecing stitch (which is the running stitch combined with an occasional back-stitch). Run three or four stitches on to the needle at a time, pull the needle through and start

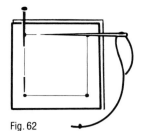
Fig. 62

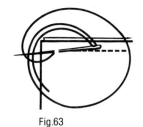
Fig.63

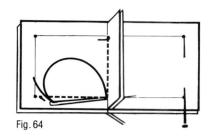
Fig. 64

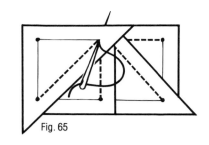
Fig. 65

the next set of running stitches. Sew three to four stitches to a centimetre.
☐ Finish with a double stitch and a figure-eight knot (Fig. 63).
☐ Cut the thread about 5 mm away from the knot.
☐ Sew the pattern pieces together to form units, matching corresponding seamlines and pin the corresponding dots (Fig. 64). Where seams cross, sew with a running or piecing stitch. Do not sew in the seam allowances (Fig. 65).

Piecing order for the single-seam method. To use this method it is necessary to be able to analyse a block and break it up into pattern pieces, and build it up again into units until all pieces have been sewn together.
☐ First, look for a seamline that runs through the block. In some cases this line is hidden because a mitred corner has been used.
☐ This line is the last seamline which will be sewn (Fig. 66).
☐ Find another seamline that runs

through *in this unit* — the second-last seamline to be sewn. Keep on breaking up units until only single pieces are left.
The piecing order of every block is given at the top of a pattern.

Example of piecing order for *Protea barbigera* (Fig. 66)
Protea barbigera (p. 9) is a slanted protea block that has a diagonal seam running through the middle dividing the block into two triangles.
Divide the triangle in further units and piece it together as follows:
Unit no. 1: (H3 + H1) + G1
Unit no. 2: (G3 + B1)
Unit no. 3: (G5 + B3)
Unit no. 4: (G7 + L1) + G9
After piecing single units, units are sewn together (1 + 2 + 3 + 4), keeping the same order for the other half of the design. The diagonal seam should be sewn by hand, matching corresponding seams exactly.

Example of piecing order for *Protea rubropilosa* (Fig. 67)
Protea rubropilosa (p. 20) is a slanted protea block. The units to be worked together are concealed by two mitred corners. In other words, there is not a line running through the whole block. Firstly the two mitred corners should be cut and the units will become clear.

Piecing order of units:
Unit no. 1: G9 + (G7 + L5 + L7) + (G5 + L1 + L3)
Unit no. 2: Repeat for the other side.
Unit no. 3: [(G3 + B5) + B1 + H1] + G1
Unit no. 4: Repeat unit 3 for the other side of the pattern.
Unit no. 5: (B9 + B7 + B11) + B13
Unit no. 6: Repeat unit 5 for other side.
Unit no. 7: (H3 + B4) + (B3 + B15)
Now put separate units together:
Unit 7 + 6 + 5 with mitred corner.
Unit 3 + 4 on the above with mitred corner.
Unit 1 + 2 on the above with mitred corner.

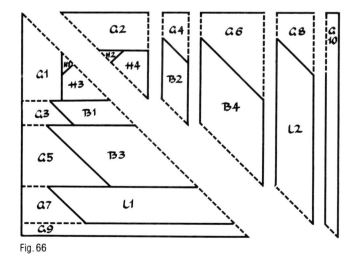
Fig. 66

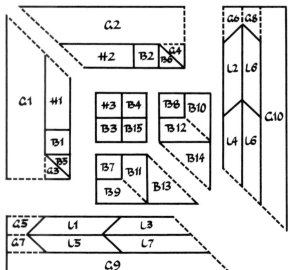
Fig. 67

45

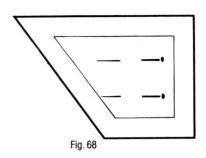
Fig. 68

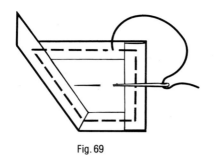
Fig. 69

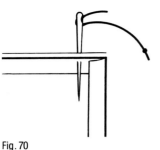
Fig. 70

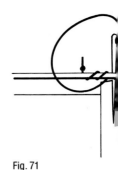
Fig. 71

2. The inlay method

In this method, fabric pieces are cut out with seam allowances and basted on to paper without a seam allowance. Two basted pieces are oversewn together. The success of this method depends on the accuracy with which paper pieces are cut out and how inconspicuously and accurately these pieces can be sewn together. It is time-consuming, but very accurate, and has the advantage that basted pieces can be laid together like a jig-saw puzzle before they are sewn, making it easy to spot and replace an offensive fabric choice.

When using this method it is not necessary to piece the background of the block. Only the protea motif is pieced and then appliquéd on to the background fabric. For the leucospermum pattern this method only must be used.

Piecing order for the inlay method. Paper patterns are cut exactly according to the templates. Use a photocopy machine to eliminate drawings. For the overall leucospermum design the patterns can be drawn on to one page of isometric paper, this paper photocopied ten times, and each of these photocopies stapled on to as many as six pages, thus enabling you to cut out enough papers for a whole quilt in a short time.

Method:
☐ Pin the paper piece on to the wrong side of the fabric piece, fold the seam allowances over the paper and baste firmly (Fig. 68 and Fig. 69).
☐ Use a fine needle and tacking thread. Start with a knot in the middle of one of the seams, make a double stitch and work along the straight grain.
☐ End the tacking thread with a double stitch in the centre (Fig. 69). When folding corners, use your needle to make

a perfect fold. Do not try to fold away extra fabric when acute angles are tacked. This can easily be folded away when the appliquéing has been done. These fabric-covered paper pieces are then oversewn together, keeping right sides together (Fig. 70-76).

☐ Use quilting thread or thread covered with beeswax and a ("between") quilting needle. Start with a single knot a little way from the corners (Fig. 70) and oversew three stitches backwards (Fig. 71), matching the corners exactly. Oversew the whole seam (Fig. 72) and match the other corners exactly. Work backwards again for three stitches (Fig. 73), ending with a double stitch (Fig. 74) of which the last movement ends with a figure-eight knot (Fig. 75). Cut off the thread, leaving a tail of 1 cm. All the pieces of the whole protea motif should be pieced like this.

If all the paper patterns are not cut accurately, or if different thicknesses of fabric are used, corresponding seams will not match. It is therefore most important to match corners perfectly, allowing extra fabric fullness to be sewn away in the middle of the specific seam.
☐ Tack the pieced protea motif on to the background. Appliqué it without removing the paper patterns. The appliquéing can be done in two ways: with the appliqué stitch which is almost an overcasting stitch (Fig. 76), or a blind stitch (Fig. 77). The stitches must be almost invisible.
☐ After the appliquéing has been done, the protea should be pressed carefully. The background behind the protea should be cut away, leaving a 6 mm seam on the background. Pull out the tacking threads of the pieced protea and remove paper pieces. Press carefully on the wrong side

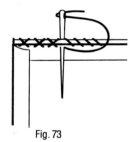
Fig. 72

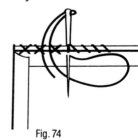
Fig. 73

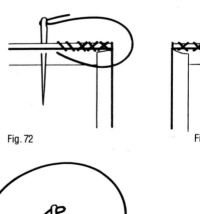
Fig. 74

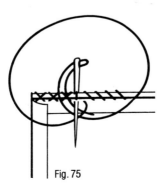
Fig. 75

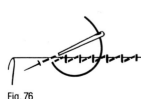
Fig. 76

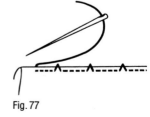
Fig. 77

Plate 11. Centre-piece of a medallion quilt, Persian rag (36 cm as well as 18 cm blocks). Hilda Hofmeyr.

once again. This will give you a perfect block which can be used with other blocks made by another method.

3. The folding-over method (Log-cabin method)

According to this method, piecing is not done in units, but starts in the centre and continues outwards. Each piece is sewn separately, folded over and the next piece sewn on to the previous one and folded over again. The whole block should be completed in this way. All piecing can be done on a light-weight base fabric on which pattern lines are marked to ensure accuracy. If a base fabric is not used, seam lines should be marked on every fabric piece. The disadvantage of using a base fabric is that a large bed quilt becomes too heavy to manage during the quilting process because of the extra layer of fabric. Even so, it is advisable to use the base fabric until the method has been mastered.

Only two pattern blocks in this book are designed for the folding-over method: *Protea caffra* (p. 18) and the protea bud (p. 19). These two blocks have relatively few pattern pieces and should not be used on blocks larger than 24 cm square. The 18 cm-size in which they are printed is the recommended one.

Method:
☐ As for all patterns, the pattern must first be redrawn according to the desired size, using the squared paper provided, and duplicated.
☐ Punch a little hole through the paper

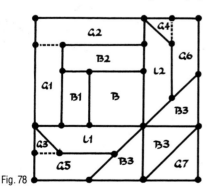

Fig. 78

on every crossing on the second drawing, using a thick needle (Fig. 78).
☐ Cut a square from any light-weight

cotton base fabric, 2 to 3 cm larger than the desired block size.
☐ Use masking tape to fix the paper pattern over the fabric.
☐ Use a soft marking pencil (2B) and make dots through the little holes of the paper on to the fabric.
☐ Remove the paper pattern and join the pencil dots to transfer the pattern on to the fabric.
☐ Lengthen all lines on the base fabric beyond the crossing point to assist with the sewing.

Piecing order for folding-over method. Cut out fabric pieces with 6 mm seam allowances. If the pattern has been traced on to the base fabric, it is not necessary to mark stitching lines. If the no-base method has been used, templates must be made and marked on all fabric pieces. Also mark the corner points with a dot.

Method:
☐ Pin piece B, right side up, in position in the centre of the base fabric.
☐ Pin piece B1, wrong side up, on top of B so that the corresponding seams meet (Fig. 79).

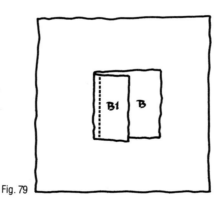

Fig. 79

☐ Follow the extended marked line on the base fabric and sew over the seam allowance. Fold piece B1 over to cover the raw edge of the seam, pressing it flat with the finger and using a pin to keep it in position. Continue now with B2, G1, G2, and so on in the same way until all the pieces have been folded over and sewn in position (Fig. 80). See p. 18 (*Protea caffra*).

When you come to piece B3, first sew the three pieces together with an open

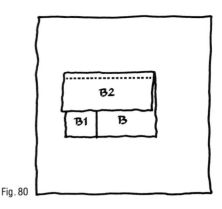

Fig. 80

seam, then treat them as one piece and sew on to the block in the same way as before.

If 24 or more blocks are going to be made, it is realistic to work in units of four, sewing everything by machine. Instead of cutting pattern pieces, cut strips of fabric the desired width and length as needed. Use the rotary cutter and plastic strips to save a great deal of time.

PIECING WITH THE SEWING MACHINE

The choice between whether an article is going to be hand-sewn or machine-sewn depends entirely on personal preference, ability and the circumstances under which the sewing is going to be done. It is easier to sew small pieces by hand, while long seams are faster by machine. Long diagonal seams are more accurate by hand. Hand-piecing is perfect for in-between moments while machine sewing can be done only at specific times and in a specific place. Hand piecing ensures a supple article while a machine-pieced article is stiffer. Personally, I find hand piecing much easier, more accurate and relaxing.

Block patterns for both single-seam and folding-over methods are suitable for machine piecing.

Hints for machine piecing
☐ The sewing machine must be in perfect working order and fitted with a new, very fine needle.
☐ Use the same sewing thread, preferably mercerized cotton, on the top and bottom.
☐ Check the width of the machine foot

and cut all seam allowances accordingly. Usually they are 6 mm or 7 mm.

☐ Sewing lines need not be marked on pieces, if the cutting is done accurately.

☐ Special care must be taken to prevent puckering when sewing. Sew eight to ten stitches to 2,5 cm. When many pattern pieces are sewn it is a good idea to chain sew, cutting thread in between only afterwards. This method saves a lot of time. Do not sew backwards.

☐ Press seam allowances while sewing, preferably towards the darker fabric. Sometimes it is necessary to press seams open to prevent bulkiness. When seams cross, pressing must be done in such a way that bulkiness is prevented.

☐ When sewing over crossed seams, the bottom seam allowance must be pushed forwards and the top seam allowance backwards by lifting the pressure foot to sew a corner accurately.

☐ Use pins to match seams, putting the heads towards the raw edge so that they can be pulled out easily. Never pin through seam allowances.

☐ When six or eight seams meet, it is better not to sew over these crossings, but to continue from the other side. This ensures that the corners match.

☐ Cut loose thread ends continually within 5 mm of the stitch to make sure that loose ends are not sewn down.

☐ Do not bother to cut corners or ravels during the sewing process. Leave this until just before the top is finished.

GRAIN DIRECTION

With small fabric pieces cut on evenly woven cotton fabric, the direction of the lengthwise and crosswise grain is not important, though it is helpful to keep the bias in mind. When pieces get larger or when border strips are cut, the direction of the grain becomes important. It is better to cut strips and large oblong pieces on the lengthwise grain running with the selvedge of the fabric.

It is important that the edge of a block runs with the straight grain of the fabric and never on the bias. This must be kept in mind especially when a diagonal layout is used and the edge of the quilt is filled in with triangles. The straight grain must run on the border, while the blocks themselves are also on the straight grain. (Please note the arrows on the quilt designs to ensure the correct grain direction is followed.)

Exceptions: For striped fabrics or border prints the direction of the stripe is more important than the direction of the grain. Oblong pieces usually look better with stripes running lengthwise, especially a protea leaf or bract.

For fabrics with directional prints, cut pieces according to the growth direction of the protea, and ignore the grain.

For protea designs consisting of many small squares or diamonds, cut as many seams as possible on the straight grain.

Plate 12. Centre-piece of a bed quilt. Irene van Tonder.

V QUILTING

The beauty and value of a quilt lies in the quality of the quilting. This is the process in which the three layers of a quilt — the pieced top, the batting and the back — are sewn together with a quilting stitch. The quilting influences the texture of the quilt and must be seen as an integral part of the quilt. The loftiness of the batting decides the puffiness of the unquilted areas — in contrast to the indents formed by the quilting stitch. This is then responsible for the subtle light reflection which gives the dimensional quality to a quilt.

The quilting too is responsible for the durability of the article, holding the three layers of fabric together, preventing friction and strain on the seams. Be prepared to spend as much, and even more, time and planning on the quilting than on the piecing.

PREPARING FOR QUILTING

The careful preparation of the quilt top, batting and back ensures that the quilting process will run smoothly and that the quilt will be square and neat. The three layers must first be sandwiched. It helps for two people to do this job together.

Basting
☐ Sew two oblong tubes of fabric on to the shortest sides of the quilt top which will be rolled on to the rolling beams.
☐ Neaten the quilt top, ensuring that there are no loose threads or ravels hanging on the wrong side. Press all the seams and make sure that no dark seams show through light pieces. Cut excess fabric away, especially where seams add to the bulkiness of the crossing.

☐ Shake the quilt top to get rid of loose ravels and threads.
☐ Fold the top into four and mark the middle of each side with a pin or coloured thread.
☐ Press the quilt on the wrong side avoiding extra thicknesses. Use a steam iron or ordinary iron with a pressing cloth or a steam press.
☐ Leave the quilt to make sure that all seams lie flat and that it is thoroughly dry.
☐ Push the two roller sticks into the tubes on both sides, fix with thumb tacks and stretch the quilt on a carpet or a big table, right side under. Make sure that the quilt is square on these poles, measuring the fixed length.
☐ Spread the batting over the wrong side of the quilt top, making sure that no seams turn while spreading it. (The batting should have been opened up for at least 12 hours so that it lies perfectly flat.) The batting should extend beyond the quilt top on all four sides.
☐ If the batting is not wide enough, splice the two pieces of batting together by overlapping half of a 10 cm strip of batting on one edge, half of a 10 cm strip on the other edge without extra thickness (Fig. 81).

Fig. 81

☐ The back usually consists of two widths of fabric pieced together. Rather than one seam straight down the middle, it works better to have two seams.
☐ Cut the back a few centimetres larger than the quilt top to allow for any possible stretching.
☐ Fold the back in four and again mark the middle of the sides.

☐ Spread the back, right side up, over the batting, making sure that the centre marks on both quilt top and back correspond, and the backing fits precisely.
☐ Use a sharp needle and basting thread (no. 120) and start basting from the centre of the quilt, with the straight grain, outwards in four directions (south, west, north, east) and then diagonally (Fig. 82). From then basting is done systematically from the centre so as to leave no area bigger than the open hand unbasted.
☐ Make sure that all extra fullness is moved outwards, ending off each row of basting by stitching a few smaller stitches, but not doing any double stitching. Pin the open edges together with long pins.

Using a frame
Quilting can be done in different ways, with or without a frame, on the lap or with a quilting hoop. The exact stitch and even the way it is worked will depend on personal preference and will be affected by the type and thickness of the batting and fabric used for the top and the quilt back.

The use of a frame is to be recommended because quilting will proceed faster, more than one person can work at the same time and stitching will be more even. As it also cuts down on handling, it is easy to form even stitches, and the quilt will be square.

How to work on a frame (Fig. 83)
☐ After the basting has been done carefully, scroll the quilt inwards towards the quilt back on the roller beams until about 40 cm of quilt is left in the centre.
☐ Make sure that the quilt is rolled in such a way that it is not skew or creased.

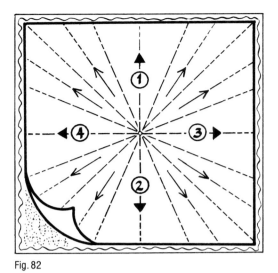

Fig. 82

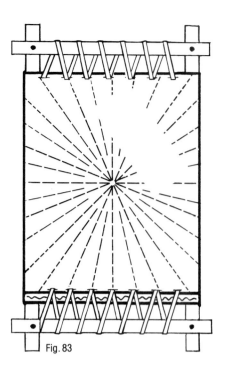

Fig. 83

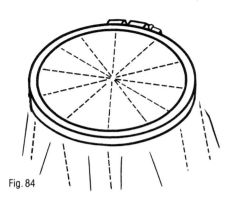

Fig. 84

□ Fix the two straining beams on both corners of one of the roller beams and then on the other two sides with "G" clamps.

□ Use a long strip of fabric or binding to stretch the sides of the quilt on to the straining beams. Wind the strips around the roller beams and pin on to the quilt. Pin at about 8-10 cm intervals. After completing the quilting within the exposed area, reveal a fresh section, unpinning the taped sides and rolling the completed part on to one of the beams. Secure the sides again as before.

□ With the quilt stretched on to the frame, it can easily be supported by trestles, chair backs or even a windowsill at a comfortable working height,

No-frame method. If lap quilting is to be executed, basting should be done more carefully. Roll up the quilt and lay it on a table to prevent the weight of the quilt from distorting the quilting stitches.

Quilting hoop (Fig. 84). The use of an oval or round quilting hoop has the advantage that the quilt can be easily moved, and it only requires a small working space. The hoop can be supported by a stand on a table or on the lap. Attention should be given to keeping the tension of the exposed area even.

The quilting stitch
The traditional quilting stitch is an ordinary running stitch worked by hand in such a way as to form an indent which forms a little shadow on the top. The stitch itself may be nearly invisible or quite visible. It may be the same size at the front and the back, or smaller at the front and larger at the back, or large at the front and small at the back, depending on the quilter's preference. It is noteworthy that no two people work a certain type of stitch exactly the same.

Decorative stitching can be used as well, depending on the effect required. The problem with decorative stitching is that the thread is usually thick and that it is difficult to sew through all the layers of fabric. The typical indent is also invisible.

Quilting on a *sewing machine* can be done on a less valuable article where suppleness is not a sought-after quality. The article will be stiffer and the stitching lines will show as lines and not as indents. If quilting is done by machine the blind hem attachment should be used.

A quilt can also be *knotted* instead of having it quilted. A square knot is tied every 10-14 cm apart. This can be done on the lap, though it is easiest on a frame. It is especially appropriate for very thick battings and in less valuable articles or where fabrics are too thick to sew fine stitches.

The quilting stitches must be sewn evenly and must be the same size. It takes a lot of practice to master the basic movements to ensure a rhythmic working action, but once mastered, the work will be sheer pleasure. The tension of the stitches is also important.

QUILTING

□ Begin a 50 cm quilting thread with a knot, using a no. 7 or 8 quilting needle.
□ Insert the needle in the top of the quilt about one centimetre from the desired beginning of the quilting line. Do not go through all of the thicknesses. Keep the needle in the batting and pull it through where the quilting should begin.
□ Pull the needle until the knot slips through the top, burying itself in the batting. If the knot should pull through, make a slightly larger knot and try again.
□ Make one backstitch before settling into the quilt stitch (Fig. 85).

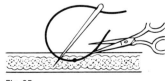

Fig. 85

☐ Start the quilting by holding the needle with the thumb and forefinger. Settle the eye of the needle into a hollow in the thimble on the right-hand middle finger. Position the needle and take away the thumb and forefinger, pushing the needle with the thimble vertically down through all the layers of the quilt until you feel it against the left-hand index finger under the quilt. Guide the needle back into the quilt, using the thimble on the right hand, manipulate the needle in a see-saw manner so that three to five stitches are made before it is pulled through again with the thumb and forefinger (Fig. 86).

To prevent the forefinger on the left hand from being pricked, use a flat top thimble or a special quilting metal device for this purpose.

When ending the thread, make a backstitch with 5 to 10 cm of thread remaining in the needle. Then make a loop of thread near the fabric. Draw the needle into the fabric where the next stitch should be taken (Fig. 87), carefully pulling the knot into the batting again, burying it, and bringing the needle back to the top of the fabric about 2 cm away in a pieced seam, if possible. Pull the needle through and trim the thread close to the fabric.

If there is a seam nearby, you may hide a few tiny backstitches in the seam for extra security.

Hints for hand quilting. To master quilting takes practice. Special hand muscles must be developed and a special eye-hand co-ordination must be learned. Try from the outset to do it in the right way, even if it feels slow and uncomfortable at first. It will eventually develop into a rhythmic movement that can be executed so quickly that it becomes pure pleasure and will repay all those time-consuming practice sessions.

A few hints:
☐ The quilt must not be pulled too tight on the frame, neither must it be loose enough to allow the layers to shift.
☐ Change your body's position regularly. You should maintain a comfortable arm's length from the frame.
☐ Always work from the centre outwards preventing any extra fabric fullness from being captured.

Extra fullness must always be moved outwards.
☐ Keep a pair of light-weight scissors on hand to trim threads.
☐ Start a quilting session with a straight line or on a print until a rhythmic movement of the hands and eyes is reached before quilting on solids or attempting intricate patterns.
☐ Ideally, it should be impossible to see the beginning or ending of any line of quilting.
☐ The correct tension of stitches can be judged by sliding a pin behind a stitch and making sure that the thread does not lie loosely. If the pin cannot be pushed in behind a stitch, it is too tight. The finer the stitch, the finer the pin to be used. Too tight a tension will result in the quilt puckering, while too loose a stitch will result in the top quilting looking undefined or sloppy.

☐ Always try to start work in the 02h00 position from right to left and somewhat towards you.
☐ For circles, start with a double length of thread without a knot. Start in the 02h00 position and work downwards to the 07h00 position. Then do the other half the same way, with the thread hanging loose.
☐ Use a few needles and work as far as is comfortable with one before changing position and picking up the next (threaded) needle. If someone helps with the threading it saves a lot of time.
☐ Work a backstitch, showing as an ordinary single quilting stitch on both sides, before turning a corner. This prevents a little bubble forming at the corner.
☐ Avoid unnecessary beginning and finishing points by sliding the needle through the batting to the next line. Start the next line with a small backstitch on the quilt top to prevent puckering.
☐ It is necessary to plan a route for every pattern on paper before you start quilting. Each pattern and even each quilting direction needs its own route.

Stuffed or trapunto *quilting*
For this type of quilting, the quilting stitch is sewn through two layers of fabric, without an overall batting. The stuffing is added afterwards between quilted areas. Originally, this was done only on all-white cotton and was considered the final test of workmanship because every stitch had to be perfect. There are three variations on this theme:

Trapunto motifs consist of very small quilted areas. The stuffing is then added from the back by pushing the threads of the backing aside gently, stuffing the motif and arranging the threads in position again.

For the *Italian* variation areas to be stuffed are stitched in parallel lines. Stuffing, usually a very thick thread like rug wool, is threaded into an embroidery needle and slid between the quilted lines.

For *shadow quilting* a coloured fabric is used instead of the batting. Motifs are cut out from the coloured fabric and tacked into position on to the back. The top of the quilt is a very thin, sheer

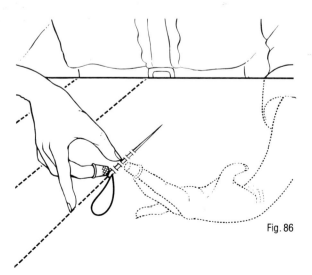

Fig. 86

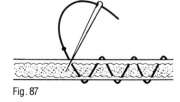

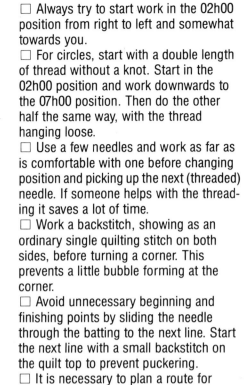

Fig. 87

Plate 13. Part of a bed quilt design (260 cm x 260 cm). June Kruger.

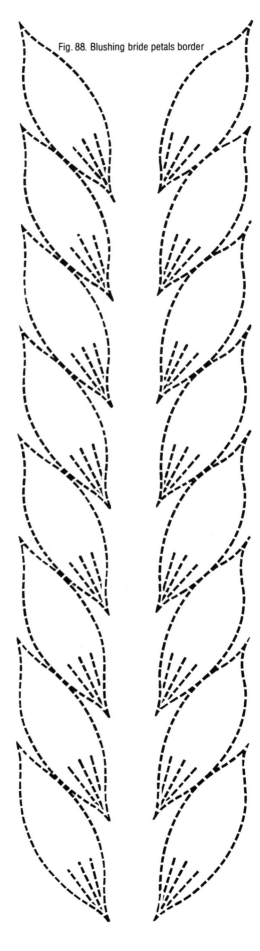

Fig. 88. Blushing bride petals border

cotton. Quilting is done around the motifs.

The three quilting variations described above can be used successfully in quilting compositions.

THE USE OF QUILTING DESIGNS

A variety of quilting designs are included (Fig. 88; 93-123). They are especially suitable for protea quilts but can be used with any other block or quilt designs. All patterns can be enlarged or reduced to fit specific sizes. If an enlargement makes the pattern seem too empty, double lines can be quilted. Enlargements can easily be drawn on to 7,5 mm and 1 cm squared paper pads, available from stationery shops or the addresses on p. 8.
NB: the printed designs were designed on a 5 mm square or isometric grid.

Transferring designs to fabric
Try to have as few marking lines on the fabric as possible. However, designs that need to be marked should be done as inconspicuously as possible with a very sharp marking pencil or tailor's tracing paper. Whatever marker is used, it is always wise to test it first to make sure marks can be easily removed from the fabric you are using.

Quilting designs can be transferred on to the fabric in different ways, either before the quilt sandwich is made or afterwards. The advantage of doing it on the quilt top is that it can be done very accurately. The advantage of doing it while it has already been sandwiched and tacked on the frame is that it allows for more creative work, and quilting designs can be added or omitted as the quilting proceeds.

Whichever the technique of transferring designs and at what stage it is done largely depends on the individual and the specific quilt, the amount of quilting to be done and the intricacies of the pattern.

The easiest and fastest way to transfer designs is to use a *light table*. One can easily be made by using a piece of glass, covering the sharp edges with masking tape and putting it on a sliding-leaf table. Place a source of light directly underneath.

You could also use a *glass top table*. Place a light underneath and fix the quilting design on the glass top with masking tape. Put the quilt top over the design, secure with tape and simply trace the design on to the quilt top using a fine pencil. This method is especially suitable for fabrics of light colour. For darker fabrics the design must first be traced on to black or brown paper and stitched along these lines with the sewing machine. When the paper is placed on the glass top, the light will show through the dotted lines. The pattern can now be copied on to the quilt top with a light pencil.

Designs can be cut out on *templates*. Templates are made of firm paper, index-card thickness, on which the quilting design is glued and cut out. Position the template and trace around the edges on to the fabric. Holes or V-slits can be made to indicate further instructions or details. Sometimes it might be necessary to make a "window" in the template to trace designs on the inside as well. For intricate designs more than one template can be made so as to be able to fill in detail. Multiple-size plastic templates and transparent stencils are also available.

Use a *ruler, a plastic strip or transparent grid rulers* to transfer straight lines directly on to the fabric.

Dressmaker's carbon paper in white or a light colour with a tracing wheel is easy to use if motifs are not too intricate, though avoid using this for rounded areas. Tape the quilt top to the cutting board or cutting surface to hold it in place. Transfer the quilting pattern to thin paper, place dressmaker's carbon over the area to be marked and pin the motif on top of it. Carefully guide the tracing wheel around the outlines of the design. Use the rounded hook end of a small crochet hook to trace corners.

Always test the dressmaker's carbon on a swatch of the fabric to be sure it will disappear when a damp cloth or steam iron is held above the quilt top.

Masking tape in different widths is especially suitable for marking short, straight lines when the quilt is already secured on a frame. Stitch alongside the edge, remove the tape and use the same piece again until it won't stick any more.

(Keep masking tape in a plastic bag or well-sealed holder to ensure that it does not dry out before use.) Motifs can also be cut out of wider masking tape, stuck on to the fabric and quilted around the edge.

Re-usable self-adhesive templates for no-mark quilting are also available.

Designs for quilting
The quilting patterns must enhance the quilt top. The more complicated the piecing, the plainer the quilting pattern should be; the plainer the piecing, especially when solid colours are used, the greater the interest that should be added by the quilting. The judicious choice and placement of the quilting, perfectly executed, will enhance the quality of the article.

Different ways to quilt
In-the-ditch stitching is used to define the outline of pieced areas. The stitch is sewn in the seamline, thus leaving no indent and showing no stitch, though the area surrounded by the stitching is defined. This is mostly done on block and border edges. The whole protea flower can also be quilted like this, especially when the pieces are very small.

Outline stitching is the most common form of quilting. To outline, follow the shape of each fabric piece in the protea motif, 3-6 mm from the seam line, within each shape. Additional quilting lines can be added inside a piece. Outline stitching can also be used on the outside of the whole protea motif (Fig. 89).

Echo or contour stitching is quilting with parallel lines, 6-10 mm apart, following the outside shape of the motif until the space is filled. It is a very pleasing and an easy background for the protea motif (Fig. 90). Draw these lines on paper first, making sure that you follow the natural growth direction of the protea flower, and that all lines are the same distance apart. Sew from the stem upwards and never around the whole flower.

Stippling stitching is done in rows of waves, 3-4 mm apart, following the outline of the flower. The tiny stitches formed in this way will give the impression that they were sewn at

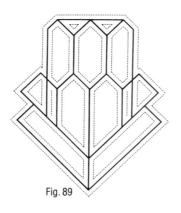

Fig. 89

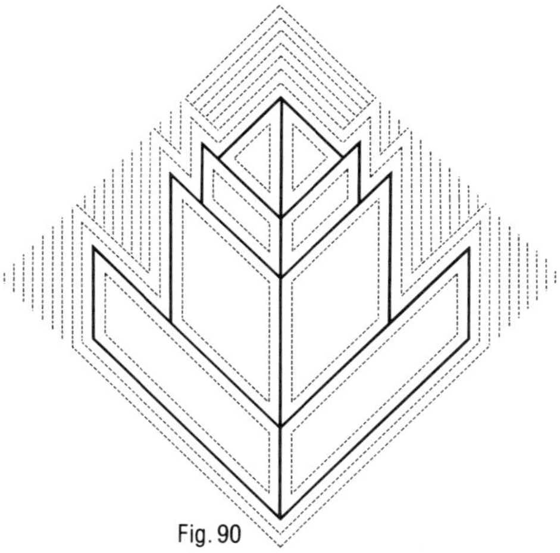

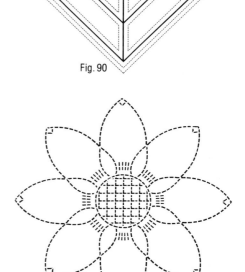

Fig. 90

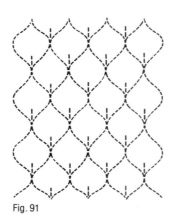

Fig. 91

Fig. 92

random, creating an overall textured area.

Filler quilting patterns are used for sewing big open areas and for the background of elaborate designs. Filler patterns must have an overall effect. Straight or curved lines are used (Fig. 91). If these lines are worked on the bias grain of the fabric, they tend to look more interesting.

Motifs for quilting are especially suitable in blocks and defined areas where no piecing is done. Realistic as well as stylised designs are suitable for this type of quilting. All the protea block patterns (Chapter 1) can be used for motif quilting. The design will show up best if the area around the motif is filled by echo quilting, or stippling or with a filler (Fig. 92).

Border designs are most useful when used on sashes and borders. They usually consist of flowing repeated patterns which can end sharply before a corner is turned or flow into the corner

and make a turn in a symmetrical way. if the border design has a definite direction, it should turn in the centre of the side, and turn again symmetrically in the corner.

Quilting on the outlines of a printed motif is an easy way to quilt. It is especially useful on border prints, and eliminates the marking process.

The quilt patterns on the following pages are meant to inspire original designs by indicating how the basic designs could be varied to create an infinite range of patterns. Keep in mind that these patterns were all designed on squared paper marked in 5 mm blocks and may be traced directly on to the same size grid. Any original pattern can easily be enlarged to one and a half times or twice its size by copying the basic pattern lines on to a 7,5 mm or 1 cm grid respectively.

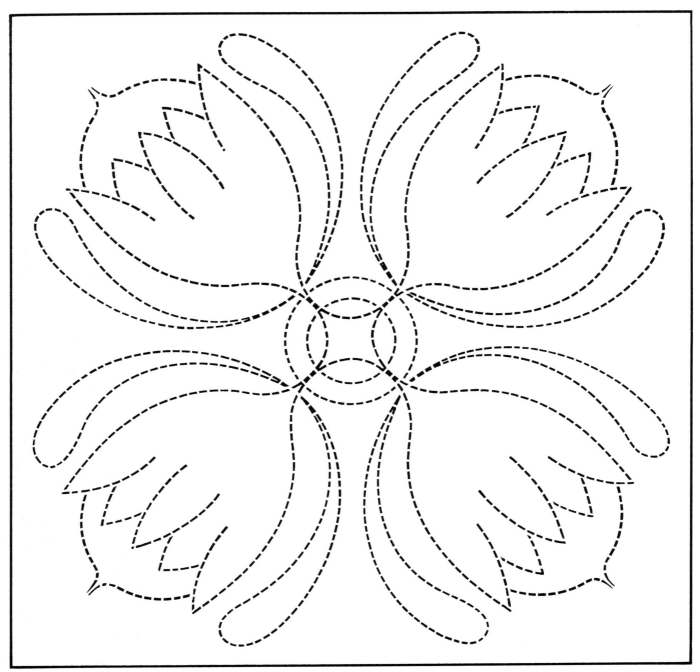

Fig. 93. Magnificent square

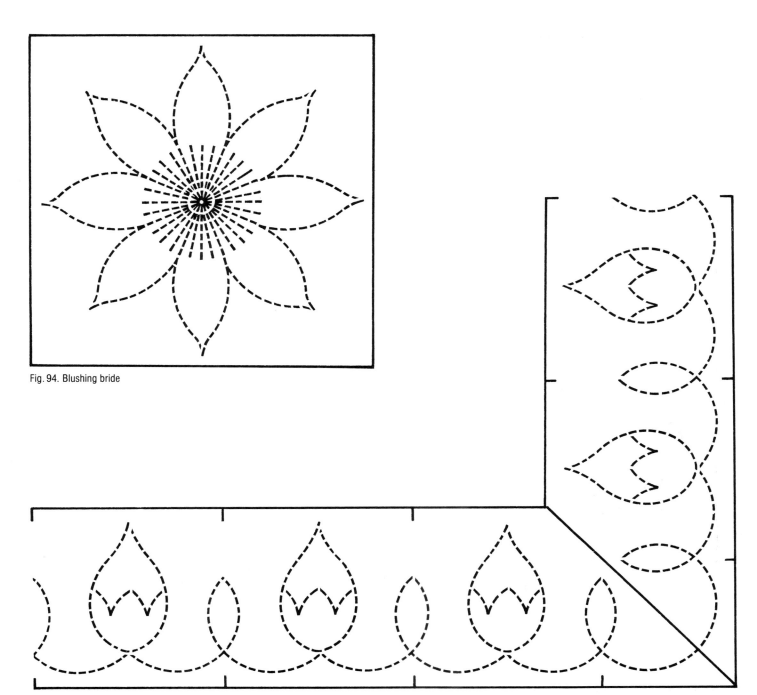

Fig. 94. Blushing bride

Fig. 95. Plume border

Fig. 96. Drakensberg circle (isometric)

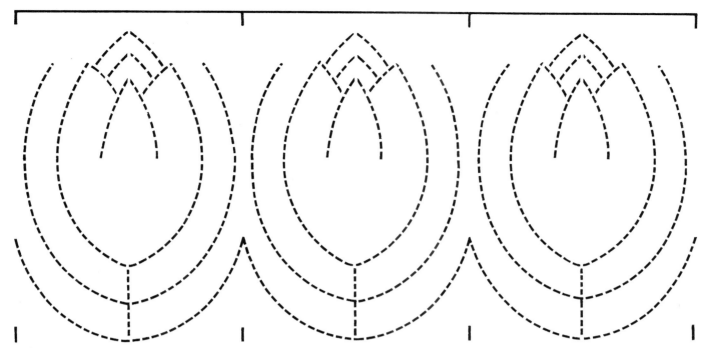

Fig. 97. Drakensberg border

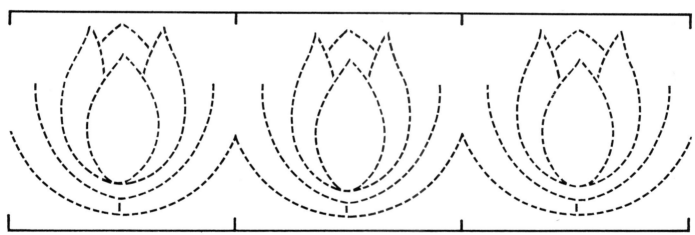

Fig. 98. Sunshine bush border

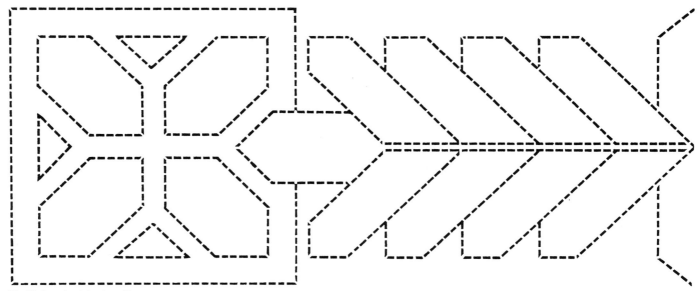

Fig. 99. Sugarbush border with square corner

Fig. 100. Golden tips crown

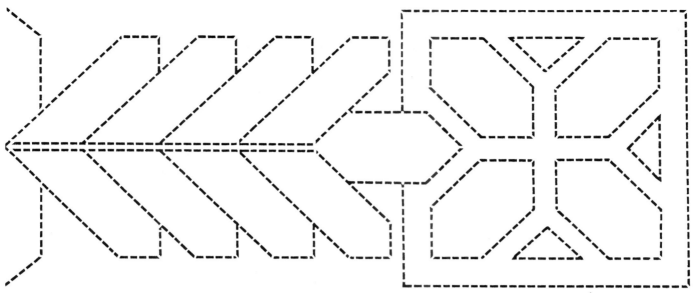

Mirror image of Fig. 99. (Turn pattern around in middle of border so that square corners are placed in corners of quilt. Insert leaves to reach appropriate border length)

Fig. 101. Spice cone

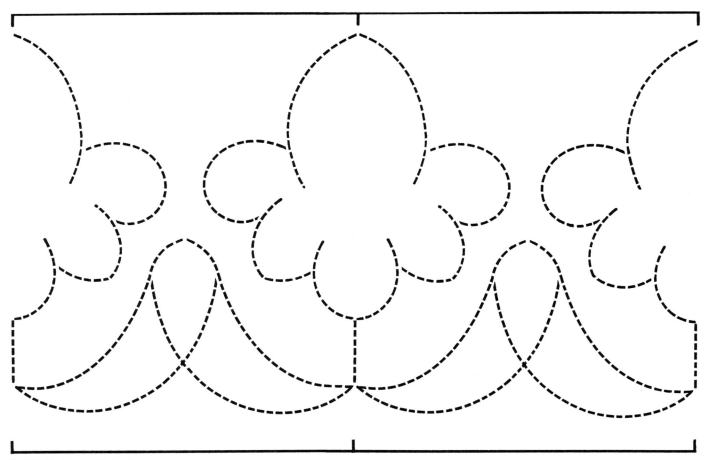

Fig. 102. *Protea punctata* border

Fig. 103. Marsh rose border. (Extend pattern to appropriate border length by inserting leaves in pairs)

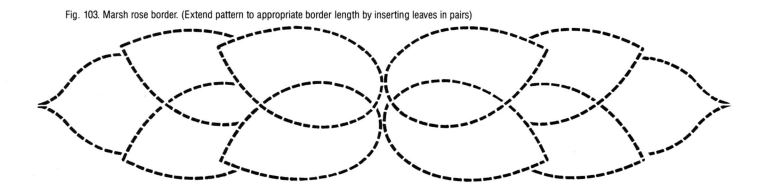

Fig. 104. *Protea punctata* square

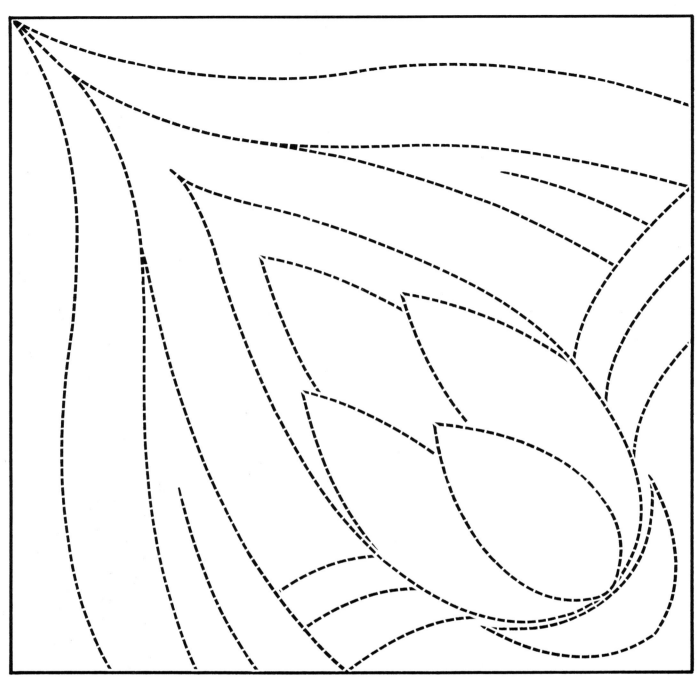

Fig. 105. Silvertree-top: quarter of 36 cm-block

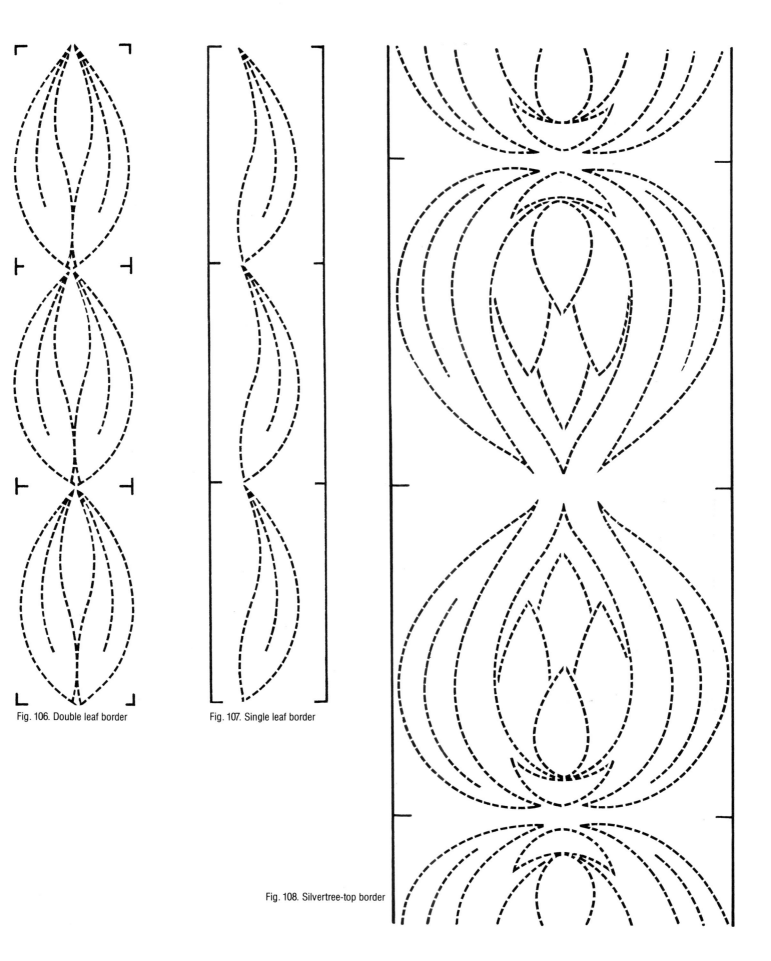

Fig. 106. Double leaf border

Fig. 107. Single leaf border

Fig. 108. Silvertree-top border

Fig. 109. Silvertree-top square

Fig. 110. Spiral: quarter of 36 cm block

Fig. 111. Stippling

Fig. 112. Protea crown (isometric)

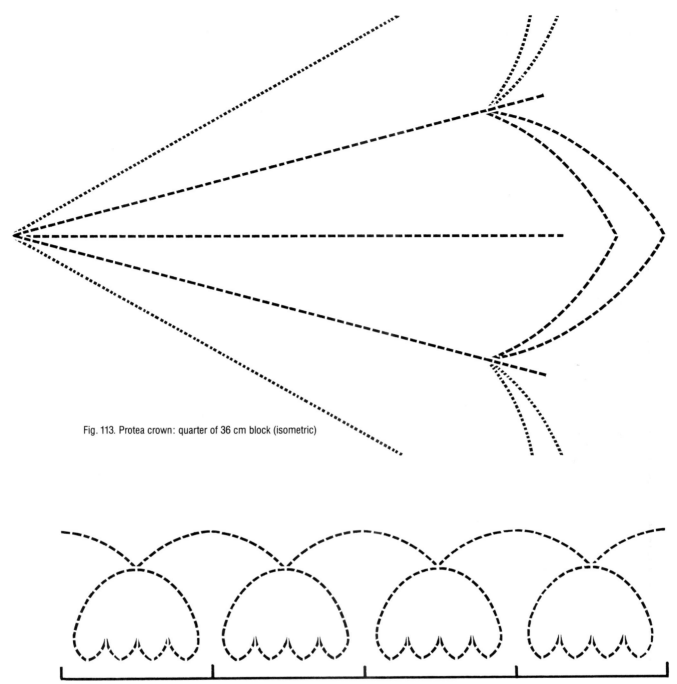

Fig. 113. Protea crown: quarter of 36 cm block (isometric)

Fig. 114. Nodding rose border

Fig. 115. Heath border

Fig. 116. Mountain rose border

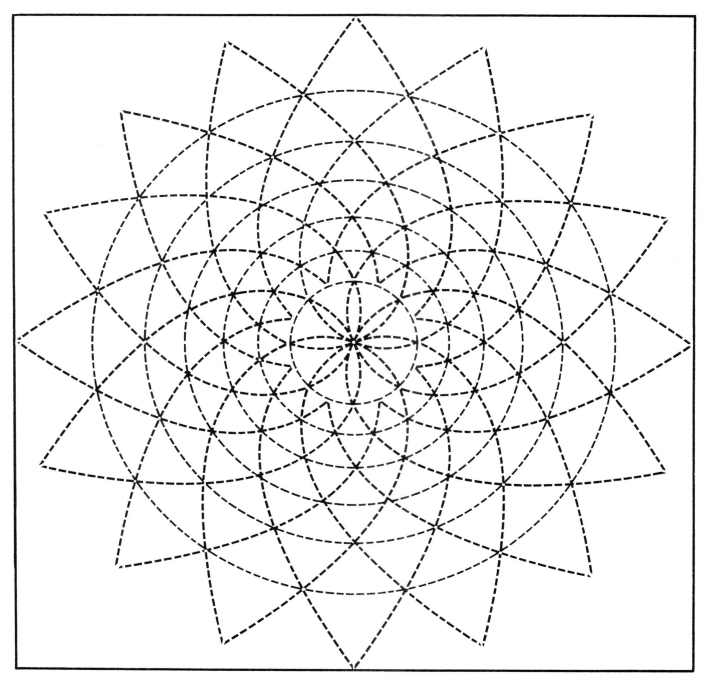

Fig. 117. Spiral

Fig. 118. Waboom square

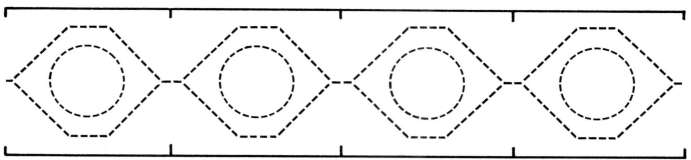

Fig. 119. Bead cone border

Fig. 120. Waboom circle: quarter of 36 cm block

Fig. 121. Overall pattern

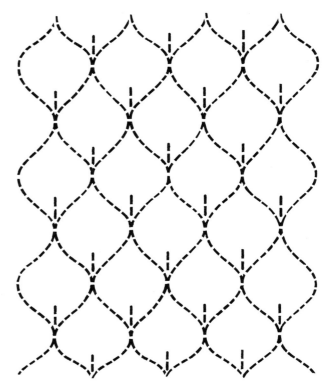

Fig. 122. Overall pattern

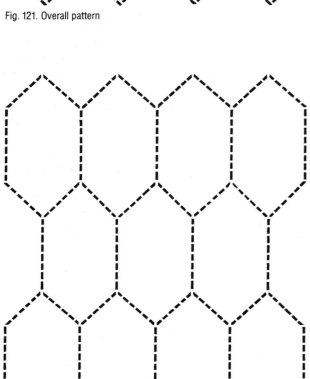

Fig. 123. Overall pattern

VI FINISHING EDGES

There are three ways to finish the edges of a quilted article: an ordinary hem which can be folded to the right or the wrong side; a slip-stitch edge which can be folded; or the easiest and most common way — a binding which can be added.

The edge must be durable and must enhance the quilt top further. Decide about the edge beforehand so that you allow the necessary fabric.

Baste the quilted sandwich along the edges before removing it from the frame, to ensure that the three layers of fabric do not shift while finishing the edges. When all the quilting is finished, trim the backing and batting to suit the specific method. Use the rotary cutter, cutting board and 60 cm plastic strips to ensure even edges.

1. The hem
☐ The top or backing that will be used for the hem should be cut at least 5 to 10 cm larger than the batting, and the part that the hem is sewn on to should be cut to the desired quilt size.
☐ Fold the hem as an ordinary dress

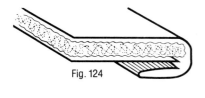

Fig. 124

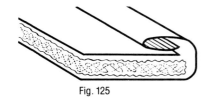

Fig. 125

hem covering the raw edges and work with a tiny blind stitch (Fig. 124 and 125).
☐ To mitre the corner, fold the seam allowance diagonally over the corner and cut the excess fabric away at the corner (Fig. 126). Fold both sides towards each

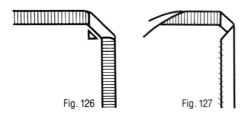

Fig. 126   Fig. 127

other using a slip-stitch to form a neat mitre on the corner (Fig. 127).
☐ After hemming, the edges can be quilted flat some 3 to 6 mm from the hem. This ensures a neat, durable edge.

2. The slip-stitch edge
This edge is especially suitable for reversible quilts and in cases where an extra binding or border will distract from the quilt design.
☐ Cut both quilt top and backing 6 mm to 1 cm larger than the desired size of the quilt.
☐ Trim the batting to the exact quilt size. (Quilting should be done to approximately 6 mm to 1 cm from from the edge or can be left until the edge is finished completely.)
☐ Fold the quilt top over the batting and fold the backing inwards as well (Fig. 128).

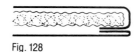

Fig. 128

☐ Baste on top of the edge, thus ensuring that sides are even.
☐ Slip-stitch the quilt back and top together.
☐ The edges can be quilted flat to give a neat appearance. Use a quilt stitch and work 3 mm from the edge fold line.

3. Binding finish
Binding is by far the most common method of finishing the edges, because it is easy to do and lasts longest. The amount of fabric needed for binding is estimated according to the width of the binding (7 to 8 cm) multiplied by the total length. This amount is then divided to fit into the meterage.

A binding is always used on the straight for straight edges and is only used on the bias when it goes around a curved edge. Then the binding should be doubled. If the binding is doubled, iron beforehand to secure the fold.
☐ Cut the quilt top, batting and back 6 mm larger than the quilt size.
☐ Tack the two layers together. This is best done while the quilt is still on the frame.
☐ Accurately position the raw edges of the double binding on top of the quilt top edges.
☐ Machine or hand sew the binding on to the edge, 6 mm from the raw edges.
☐ Fold the binding to the back or to the top of the quilt and slip-stitch it over the stitching line by hand (Fig. 129).
☐ Please note that in the case of a square corner two opposite sides of the

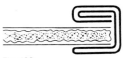

Fig. 129

quilt should be bound first (Fig. 130). The binding must be folded over the first binding at the corner and the other two sides bound by the method described above (Fig. 131).

For a curve instead of a corner a bias strip, approximately 20 cm long, is pieced on to the straight binding so that

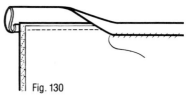

Fig. 130

the curve can be accommodated easily. The sewing is done continuously around the quilt.

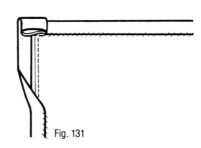

Fig. 131

Plate 14. *Protea rubropilosa*. Irene van Tonder.

Plate 15. *Protea barbigera*. June Kruger.

Plate 16 *(bottom):* Border patterns for quilting.

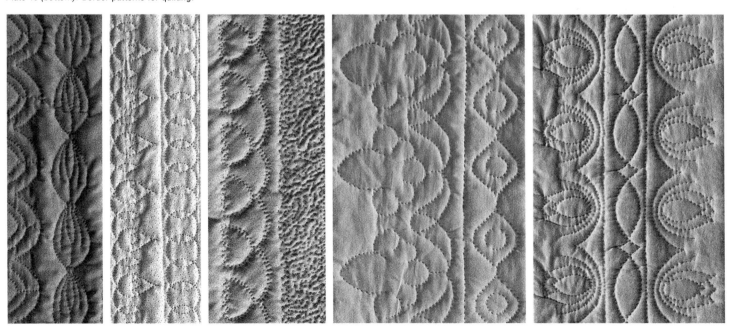

VII   SIGNING AND CARE OF QUILTS

SIGNING A QUILT

All quilts, small or large, which were made because we took pride in our work, should have a name a signature and a date on them. This is particularly important when the quilt is an original piece of work.

For quilts with protea motifs, it is also of interest to write the name of the specific protea on the block. The quilt as a whole may also be named — it is then easily referred to at an exhibition or in a private collection. If there were co-workers, or the design was copied from another piece of art, or should there be any other information of interest, write it with indelible ink on a separate piece of fabric and whipstitch it on to the back of the quilt.

Name, date and signature should not detract from the design of the quilt, and yet they should not be so inconspicuous that no one will ever see them. The scale should correspond to the size of the blocks and the article.

Different ways of marking:

□ A signature and date with an indelible laundry marker was used in the previous century even in the middle of decorative blocks. Today this method is seldom used.

□ Backstitch the information on the quilt top before it is sandwiched. Baste a piece of batting behind the area to be signed, write the specific information with a very sharp pencil and backstitch over it with quilting thread.

□ You can use quilting stitches to write the name during the quilting process, but the result is not very conspicuous.

□ Use punch stitches when the quilt is on the frame. This is time-consuming, but is the best way to do it.

□ A special gauze is available over which cross stitch can be sewn. The threads of the gauze are dampened and pulled out after sewing the stitches.

CARE OF A QUILT

As with all beautiful objects, a quilt should receive special attention and care if you wish it to last long and always look its best.

Check that the fabrics used for a quilt all have the same life expectancy. Fabric should be pre-shrunk, colour-fast and washable. Use a fabric softener in the last rinse to combat static electricity which attracts dust particles.

A bed quilt in daily use should be washed twice a year, preferably after the summer and after the winter. A wall quilt should be vacuum-cleaned regularly and will only need a wash occasionally.

Hand-wash method
Wash a quilt by hand. Depending on the size this can be done in a basin or in the bath. Use a soft detergent, previously dissolved in lukewarm water. Let the quilt soak. Never rub or wring it because threads might break and pieces can be distorted especially if quilting was done sparingly. Rinse it then in clear water a few times and add some fabric softener to the last rinse. To get rid of excess water, the quilt can be carefully rolled up in towels. Spread it on a flat surface in the shade to dry.

Washing machine method
The use of a washing machine is not recommended though it is handy and initially works well. The problem is that a quilt will soon lose its liveliness and its life expectancy will be shortened markedly.

Never *dry clean* or iron a quilt.

With lots of tender loving care a quilt should bring pleasure to its maker and its owner for years to come.

BIBLIOGRAPHY

INDEX

BEYER, Jinny. *The Quilter's Album of Blocks and Borders.*
  McLean, Virginia: EPM, 1980
BEYER, Jinny. *The Art and Technique of creating Medallion Quilts.*
  McLean, Virginia: EPM, 1982
ELIOVSON, Sima. *Proteas for Pleasure — How to grow and identify them.*
  Cape Town: Howard Timmins, 1965
GUTCHEON, Beth. *The Perfect Patchwork Primer.*
  Westford, Massachusetts: The Murray Printing Company, 1973
JAMES, Michael. *The Quiltmaker's Handbook — A Guide to design and Construction.*
  Englewood Cliffs, New Jersey: Prentice-Hall, 1978
JAMES, Michael. *The Second Quiltmaker's Handbook — Creative Approaches to Contemporary Quilt Design.*
  Englewood Cliffs, New Jersey: Prentice-Hall, 1981
ROURKE, J. P. *The Proteas of Southern Africa.*
  Cape Town: Purnell, 1980
UYS, J. J. E. *Wild flowers for embroidery.*
3 Bellevue Street, Paarl: J. J. E. Uys, 1977
UYS, J. J. E. *Wild Orchids for embroidery.*
  3 Bellevue Street, Paarl: J. J. E. Uys, 1981
VOGTS, Marie. *South Africa's Proteaceae: know them and grow them.*
  Cape Town: Struik, 1982
QUILTER'S NEWSLETTER MAGAZINE.
  Wheatridge, Colorado, Leman.
SA QUILTING NEWS.
  PO Box 89456, Lyndhurst

American block method *see* Single-seam method
Amount of fabric 30
Appliqué 8, 10, 11, 12, 13, 14, 15, 16, 20, 22, 46

Back-stitch 52, 78
Background fabrics 28
Base fabric *see* Folding-over method
Basting 50
Batting 26, 28, 30, 50
Bearded protea *see* Protea barbigera
Beeswax 31, 46
Binding 75
Block combinations 24
Block patterns *see* Pattern blocks
Block layout *see* Layout of quilts
Block motif *see* Protea motif
Block size 8, 24, 32, 44
Border prints 28, 32, 37, 49
Border designs 55
Borders 28, 37; *see also* Sashes

Care of quilts 78
Colour/use of colour 26, 27
Colour combinations 27, 28
Colour of thread *see* Thread
Colouring the fabric 27
Contour stitching *see* Echo stitching
Cotton/cotton fabric 26
Cotton flannel 30
Cotton mixtures 26
Cotton polyester thread *see* Thread
Cutting knife 30
Cutting blade/knife 30
Cutting pad 30

Designs for quilting *see* Quilting designs
Double stitch 44, 45, 46
Drawings 8
Dressmaker's carbon paper 54
Dry cleaning *see* Care of quilts

Echo or contour stitching 55
Edges 75
Embroidery frame *see* Frames
English method *see* Inlay method
Equipment 30

Fabric 26, 27
Fabric collection 27
Fabric for proteas 30
Fabric markers 31
Fabric pieces 44, 46
Fibre content *see* Fabric
Figure eight knot 45
Filler quilting patterns 55
Fleece 30; *see also* Batting
Folding-over method (Log-cabin method) 8, 18, 19, 48
Frames 31, 50, 51

G-clamps 31, 51
Giant protea *see Protea cynaroides*
Glass top table 54
Glue 31
Grain of fabric 37, 44, 49

Hand-wash method 78
Hand quilting *see* Quilting
Hem 75
Hexagonal pattern 23

Inlay method (English method) 8, 10, 12, 13, 14, 15, 16, 22, 23, 46
In-the-ditch stitching 55
Iron 31, 78
Isometric paper 22, 23, 31, 55
Italian quilting 52

Knitted fabrics 26

Lap quilting 50, 51
Layout of a quilt 32, 33, 35, 36
Lengthwise grain *see* Grain of fabric
Leucospermum bud 23
Light table 54
Log-cabin method *see* Folding-over method

Machine piecing 48, 49
Masking tape 44, 54
Medallion layout *see* Layout of quilts
Mercerized cotton *see* Thread

Mitred corner 38, 75
Motifs for quilting 55

Needles 30, 51
Needlepunch 30; *see also* Batting
Needle test 26

Outline stitching 55
Overall layout *see* Layout
Overall pattern 8, 23

Paper patterns (paper pieces) 46
Paper piece *see* Paper pattern
Patterns 9-10, 12-16, 18-20, 22-23, 54, 56-74
Pattern block designs, the use of 24
Pattern blocks/block patterns 8, 9-10, 12-16, 18-20, 22-25, 30, 32, 44
Perspex strips 30, 31; *see also* Rulers
Planning of a quilt 32, 33, 35, 36, 37
Piece (piecing) 26, 44
Piecing order 9-23, 45, 46, 48, 49
Preparing fabric for quilting 26
Pressing (ironing) 31, 78
Prints 26, 27, 37; *see also* Fabric
Printed pattern 27
Protea barbigera (bearded protea) 9, 45
Protea bud 19
Protea caffra 18, 48
Protea cynaroides (giant protea) 12
Protea design 49
Protea grandiceps 15
Protea lacticolor 14
Protea longifolia 10
Protea motif/protea flowers 6, 8, 22, 78
Protea neriifolia 13
Protea punctata 16
Protea repens (sugar bush) 22
Protea rubropilosa (Wolkberg protea) 20, 45
Proteas 6
Punch stitch 78

Quilt/quilted articles 27, 28, 32, 50, 78
Quilt(ing) 50, 51, 52, 53
Quilt back 28, 50
Quilt layout *see* Layout of a quilt
Quilting on the outlines 55
Quilting designs 54, 55, 56-74; *see also* Patterns
Quilting frames *see* Frames

Quilting hoop 31, 51; *see also* Frames
Quilting needle 31, 46
Quilter's quarter 31, 44
Quilting stitch 26, 31, 51, 52, 78
Quilting thread 30, 46
Quilt top 32, 50

Rotary cutter 30
Rulers 31, 54
Running stitch 44

Sashes 32, 37; *see also* Borders
Scale 32
Scissors 30
Seam allowance 8, 37, 44, 49
Sewing machine piecing 48
Sewing gauge 31
Shadow quilting 52
Shrink 26
Single-seam method (American block method) 8, 9, 10, 12, 13, 14, 20, 44, 45
Signing a quilt 78
Slip-stitch edge 75
Solids 27; *see also* Fabric
Squared paper 8, 24, 31, 32, 44, 55
Synthetic fabric *see* Fabric
Stippling stitching 55
Straight corner 37
Strip layout *see* Layout of quilts
Stuffed or *trapunto* quilting 52
Sugar bush *see Protea repens*

Tack/tacking 50
Tailor's carbon paper 54
Tailor's chalk 31
Tailor's pins 30
Templates for piecing 44
Templates for quilting 54
Textile paints *see* Colouring of fabric
Thimbles 31, 52
Thread 30, 31, 46
Transferring designs 54
Trapunto quilting *see* Stuffed quilting

Washing machine method 78
Weaves *see* Fabric
Weight *see* Fabric
Wolkberg protea *see Protea rubropilosa*
Wrinkle resistant 26